Edward Stratemeyer

To Alaska for Gold

The fortune hunters of the Yukon, by Edward Stratemeyer - illustrted by A. B. Shute

Edward Stratemeyer

To Alaska for Gold
The fortune hunters of the Yukon, by Edward Stratemeyer - illustrted by A. B. Shute

ISBN/EAN: 9783337267889

Printed in Europe, USA, Canada, Australia, Japan

Cover: Foto ©ninafisch / pixelio.de

More available books at **www.hansebooks.com**

EDWARD STRATEMEYER'S BOOKS

Old Glory Series

Cloth   Illustrated   Price per volume $1.25.

UNDER DEWEY AT MANILA   Or the War Fortunes of a Castaway

A YOUNG VOLUNTEER IN CUBA   Or Fighting for the Single Star.

FIGHTING IN CUBAN WATERS   Or Under Schley on the Brooklyn.

UNDER OTIS IN THE PHILIPPINES   Or A Young Officer in the Tropics. (*In Press.*)

The Bound to Succeed Series

Three volumes   Cloth   Illustrated   Price per volume $1.00.

RICHARD DARE'S VENTURE   Or Striking Out for Himself.

OLIVER BRIGHT'S SEARCH   Or The Mystery of a Mine.

TO ALASKA FOR GOLD   Or The Fortune Hunters of the Yukon.

The Ship and Shore Series

Three volumes   Cloth   Illustrated   Price per volume $1.00.

THE LAST CRUISE OF THE SPITFIRE   Or Larry Foster's Strange Voyage.

REUBEN STONE'S DISCOVERY   Or The Young Miller of Torrent Bend.

TRUE TO HIMSELF   Or Roger Strong's Struggle for Place. (*In Press.*)

"Uncle Foster! Earl! Look at This!" — *Page 170*.

TO ALASKA FOR GOLD

OR

The Fortune Hunters of the Yukon

BY

EDWARD STRATEMEYER

AUTHOR OF "UNDER DEWEY AT MANILA," "A YOUNG VOLUNTEER IN CUBA"
"FIGHTING IN CUBAN WATERS," "RICHARD DARE'S VENTURE"
"OLIVER BRIGHT'S SEARCH," ETC., ETC.

ILLUSTRATED BY A. B. SHUTE

BOSTON
LEE AND SHEPARD PUBLISHERS
1899

Norwood Press
J. S. Cushing & Co.   Berwick & Smith
Norwood Mass. U.S.A.

PREFACE.

"To Alaska for Gold" forms the third volume of the "Bound to Succeed" Series. Like the preceding tales, this story is complete in itself.

The rush to the far-away territory of Alaska, when gold in large quantities was discovered upon Klondike Creek, was somewhat similar to the rush to California in years gone by. The gold fever spread to even the remotest of our hamlets, and men, young and old, poured forth, ready to endure every hardship if only the much-coveted prize might be secured. That many succeeded and that many more failed is now a matter of history, although of recent date.

In this story are related the adventures of two Maine boys who leave their home among the lumbermen, travel to California, there to join their uncle, an experienced miner, and several other men, and start on the long trip to the Klondike by way of Dyea, Chilkoot Pass, and the lakes and streams forming the headwaters of the mighty Yukon River. After many perils the gold district is reached, and here a summer and winter are passed, the former in hunting for the precious metal and the latter in a never ending struggle to sustain life until the advent of spring.

In writing the description of this new El Dorado the author has endeavored to be as accurate as possible, and has consulted, for this purpose, the leading authorities on Alaska and its resources, as well as digested the sometimes tedious, but, nevertheless, always interesting, government reports covering this subject. Regarding the personal experiences of his heroes he would add that nearly every incident cited has been taken from life, as narrated by those who joined in the frenzied rush to the new gold fields.

EDWARD STRATEMEYER.

NEWARK, N. J.,
April 1, 1899.

CONTENTS.

CHAPTER		PAGE
I.	A Letter from the West	1
II.	The Boys reach a Decision	9
III.	A False Identification	18
IV.	A Serious Set-back	27
V.	A Night in New York	36
VI.	Preparations for Departure	44
VII.	Buying the Outfits	52
VIII.	On the Way to Juneau	61
IX.	The Fate of a Stowaway	69
X.	Up the Lynn Canal	77
XI.	The Start from Dyea	85
XII.	Earl has an Adventure	93
XIII.	At the Summit of Chilkoot Pass	101
XIV.	Boat-building at Lake Linderman	109
XV.	On to Lake Bennett	118
XVI.	An Exciting Night in Camp	127
XVII.	A Hunt for Food	134
XVIII.	On to the White Horse Rapids	141
XIX.	Nearing the End of a Long Journey	149

CONTENTS.

CHAPTER		PAGE
XX.	THE GOLD FIELDS AT LAST	157
XXI.	A DAY IN DAWSON CITY	164
XXII.	DIGGING FOR GOLD	172
XXIII.	GOOD LUCK AND BAD	180
XXIV.	AN UNLOOKED-FOR ARRIVAL	187
XXV.	MORE WORK IN THE GULCHES	195
XXVI.	SLUICE BOXES AND PREPARATIONS FOR WINTER	203
XXVII.	THE END OF THE SUMMER SEASON	211
XXVIII.	SNOWED IN	219
XXIX.	WAITING AND WATCHING FOR SPRING	227
XXX.	LAST WASHINGS FOR GOLD	235
XXXI.	DOWN THE YUKON AND HOME	243

LIST OF ILLUSTRATIONS

"'Uncle Foster! Earl! look at this'" . . . *Frontispiece*

                                                              PAGE

"With a final kick the stowaway was run off the gang-plank"   72

"The water was boiling on every side" 125

"'I would like to see the prisoner, please'" 196

TO ALASKA FOR GOLD.

CHAPTER I.

A LETTER FROM THE WEST.

"It is not a question of what we should like to do, Randy; it is a question of what we must do."

"I know it, Earl. One thing is certain: the way matters stand we can't pay the quarter's rent for this timber land to-morrow unless we borrow the money, and where we are going for it I haven't the least idea."

"Nor I. It's a pity the Jackson Lumber Company had to go to pieces. I wonder where Jackson is."

"In Canada most likely. They would put him in jail if they could catch him, and he knows it."

"He ought to be put in jail!" burst out Earl, who was the elder of the two Portney brothers. "That two hundred dollars he cheated us out of would just put us on our feet. But without it we can't even pay bills now owing; and Caleb Norcross is just aching to sell this land to Dan Roland."

"If we have to get out, what are we to do?" questioned Randy, soberly. "I don't believe we can get work, unless we go into the woods as mere choppers."

"We shall have to do something," was Earl's unsatisfactory response.

The Portney brothers lived upon a small timber claim in the state of Maine. Their parents had died three years before, from injuries received in a terrible forest fire, which had at that time swept the locality. The family had never been rich, and after the sad affair the boys were left to shift for themselves. The father had owned an interest in a timber claim, and this had been sold for three hundred dollars, and with the proceeds the two brothers had rented another claim and gone to work to get out lumber for a new company which had begun operations in the vicinity.

Earl was now eighteen years of age, and Randolph, or Randy, as he was always called, was nearly seventeen. Both lads were so tall, well-built, and muscular, that they appeared older. Neither had had a real sickness in his life, and the pair were admirably calculated, physically, to cope with the hardships which came to them later.

The collapse of the new lumber combination, and the running away of its head man, Aaron Jackson, had proved a serious blow to their prospects. As has been intimated, the company owed them two hundred dollars for timber, and, as not a cent was forthcoming, they found themselves in debt, not only for the quarter's rent for the land they were working, but also at the general supply store at the village of Basco, three miles away. The boys had worked hard, early and late, to make both ends meet, and it certainly looked as if they did not deserve the hard luck which had befallen them.

It was supper time, and the pair had just finished a scanty meal of beans, bread, and the remains of a brook trout Randy had been lucky enough to catch before breakfast. Randy threw himself down on the doorstep, while Earl washed and dried the few dishes.

"I wonder if we can't get something out of the lumber company," mused the younger brother, as he gazed meditatively at his boots, which were sadly in need of soling and heeling. "They've lots of timber on hand."

"All covered by a mortgage to some Boston concern," replied Earl. "I asked Squire Dobson about it. He said we shouldn't get a penny."

"Humph!" Randy drew a deep breath. "By the way, has Squire Dobson learned anything about Fred, yet?"

"He's pretty sure Fred ran away to New York."

"I can't understand why he should run away from such a good home, can you? You wouldn't catch me doing it."

"He ran away because he didn't want to finish studying. Fred always was a wild Dick. I shouldn't wonder if he ended up by going out West to hunt Indians." Earl gave a short laugh. "He'll have his eye-teeth cut one of these days. Hullo, here comes Caleb Norcross now!"

Earl was looking up the winding road through the woods, and, gazing in the direction, Randy saw a tall, lean individual, astride a bony horse, riding swiftly toward the cabin.

"Well, boys, what's the best word?" was the sharp greeting given by Caleb Norcross, as he came to a halt at the cabin door.

"I don't know as there is any best word, Mr. Norcross," replied Earl, quietly.

"I was over to Bill Stiger's place and thought if I could see you to-night about the rent money, it would save you a three miles' trip to-morrow."

"You know we can't pay you just at present, Mr. Norcross," went on Earl. "The suspension of the lumber company has left us in the lurch."

The face of the tall, lean man darkened. "How much did they stick you for?" he asked abruptly.

"Two hundred dollars."

"Two hundred dollars! You were fools to trust 'em that much. I wouldn't have trusted 'em a cent — not a penny."

"They were well recommended," put in Randy. "Even Squire Dobson trusted them."

"That don't make no difference. I don't trust folks unless I know what I'm doing. Although I did trust you boys," added Caleb Norcross, hastily. "Your father was always a straight man."

"And we are straight, too," burst out Randy, stung by the insinuation. "You shall have your money, if only you will give us a little time."

"How are you going to get it?"

"We'll earn it," said Earl. "I am sure we can get out enough timber by fall to square accounts."

"That won't do for me — not at all. If you can't pay up to-morrow, you can consider your claim on the land at an end."

"You won't give us any time?"

"No. I can sell this whole section to Dan Roland, and I'm going to do it."

"You are very hard-hearted, Mr. Norcross," began Randy, when a look from his elder brother silenced him.

"I ain't hard-hearted — I'm only looking after my own," growled Caleb Norcross. "If I let things run, I'd do as the lumber company did — bust up. So you can't pay, nohow?"

"No, we can't pay," answered Earl.

"Then I'll expect you to quit by to-morrow noon."

Without waiting for another word, Caleb Norcross turned around his bony steed and urged him forward. In less than a minute he had disappeared in the direction whence he had come. With sinking hearts the boys watched him out of sight.

The blow they had dreaded had fallen, and for several seconds neither spoke. Then Randy, who had pulled off one boot, flung it across the kitchen floor.

"I don't care, he can have his old place," he cried angrily. "We'll never get rich here, if we stay a hundred years. I'm sick and tired of cutting timber just for one's meals!"

"It's all well enough to talk so, Randy," was the elder brother's cautious response. "But where are we to go if we leave here?"

"Oh, anywhere! We might try our luck down in Bangor, or maybe Boston."

Earl smiled faintly. "We'd cut pretty figures in a city, I'm thinking, after a life in the backwoods."

"A backwoods boy became President."

"Do you wish to try for the presidency?"

"No; but it shows what can be done; and I'm tired of drudging in the woods, without any excitement or anything new from one year's end to another. Father and mother gave us pretty good educations, and we ought to make the most of that."

"I knew he wanted to sell this land to Dan Roland," went on Earl, after a pause. "I fancy he is going to get a good price, too."

"If Roland pays over five hundred dollars he will get cheated. The timber at the south end is good for nothing."

The boys entered the cabin, lit the lamp, and sat down to discuss the situation. It was far from promising, and, an hour later, each retired to bed in a very uneasy frame of mind. They were up before daybreak, and at breakfast Earl announced his intention to go to Basco and see what could be done.

"You might as well stay at home," he continued. "It may be Norcross will come back and reconsider matters."

"Not he!" exclaimed Randy; nevertheless, he promised to remain and look over some clothing which needed mending, for these sturdy lads were in the habit of doing everything for themselves, even to sewing up rents and darning socks. Such are the necessities of real life in the backwoods.

It was a bright sunny morning, well calculated to cheer any one's spirits, yet Randy felt far from lighthearted when left alone. He could not help but wonder what would happen next.

"We've got just twenty-eight dollars and a half in cash left," he mused, as he set to work to replace some buttons on one of Earl's working shirts. "And we owe about six dollars at the general store, three dollars and a quarter for those new axes and the coffee mill, and twenty to Norcross. Heigh-ho! but it's hard lines to be poor, with one's nose continually to the grindstone. I wonder if we shouldn't have done better if we had struck out, as Uncle Foster did six years ago? He has seen a lot of the world and made money besides."

Earl had expected to be gone the best part of the forenoon, and Randy was surprised, at half-past nine, to see his elder brother returning from the village. Earl was walking along the road at the top of his speed, and as he drew closer, he held up a letter.

"It's a letter from Uncle Foster!" he cried, as soon as he was within speaking distance. "It's got such wonderful news in it that I thought I ought to come home with it at once."

"Wonderful news?" repeated Randy. "What does he say?"

"He says he is going back to Alaska,— to some new gold field that has just been discovered there,— and he wants to know if we will go with him."

CHAPTER II.

THE BOYS REACH A DECISION.

"UNCLE FOSTER is going back to Alaska?" said Randy, slowly.

"Yes; he is going to start almost immediately, too," added his elder brother. "He says the new gold diggings are something immense, and he wants to stake a claim at the earliest possible date."

Randy drew a long breath. To Alaska! What a tremendous trip that would be—five thousand miles at least! And going to such an almost unknown region would be very much like starting for the north pole.

He remembered well that his Uncle Foster had paid a visit to Alaska three years previous, sailing from San Francisco to St. Michael's Island and then taking a Yukon River steamboat to a trading camp known as Fort Cudahy. They had received several letters from him while he was up there, working for the Alaskan Transportation Company part of the time and hunting for gold whenever the opportunity offered. The letters had told of the intense cold and the suffering, and of numerous unsuccessful attempts to strike a paying claim around Fort Cudahy and at another camp, known as Circle City. His uncle had taken up several claims, but they had not panned out very well, and Mr. Portney had finally returned to the United States, to interest himself in a Colorado silver mine.

"Let me see the letter," said Randy, and Earl handed it over. "I don't see how we are to pay our way to Alaska or anywhere else," added the younger boy, ruefully, as he opened the epistle.

"You will see presently," rejoined Earl. "Read it aloud. Uncle writes such a twisted hand, I want to make sure I read aright." And Randy started at once : —

"CREEDE, COL., April 5.

"MY DEAR NEPHEWS:— I suppose you have been looking for a letter from me all winter, but the fact is I have been away from this vicinity since last December. A man from British Columbia wanted me to buy an interest in a gold mine at a settlement called Dunbar's, and I went with him. The mine proved to be worthless, and I left Dunbar's, and went to Victoria, and stayed there until three weeks ago.

"While I was in Victoria, I ran across two miners whom I had met while at Fort Cudahy in Alaska. They reported that a new gold field had been discovered farther up the Yukon River, at a place known as Klondike Creek. There had been an exodus from Circle City and Fort Cudahy to this new region, and a camp known as Dawson City had been started. They said that there were about a dozen small creeks flowing into the Klondike and into the Yukon at this point, and that it was reported and proved that the entire district was rich with gold.

"I was chary of believing the men at first, for I know only too well how many wild-cat reports start up in every mining camp. But a couple of days later I heard another report from Juneau, Alaska, to the effect that several miners had come down from this same territory by way of the lakes and Chilkoot Pass, and had brought with them over thirty-five thousand dollars in nuggets and gold dust, taken out of a place called Hunker's Creek, which runs into the Klondike.

"From these reports, and from others which are floating around, I am convinced that they have at last struck the rich vein of yellow metal which I always believed would be located there, and I am now making preparations to try my luck again in that territory, and if you two boys want to go along and think you can stand the climate, which is something awful for nine months in the year, I'll see you through. I do not know how you are fixed for cash, but I have been lucky in Colorado, and I will pay all expenses, providing you will agree to remain with me for two years, working as I work, for a one-half interest in all our discoveries — that is, a one-quarter interest to each of you and a one-half interest to myself. The expense of a year's trip to Alaska by the route we shall take, over the mountain pass, will be between six and eight hundred dollars each, for we shall have to take nearly all our outfits — clothing, tools, and provisions — along.

"I am now on the point of starting for San Francisco, and shall arrive there probably before this letter reaches you. My address will be the Palace Hotel, and I wish you to telegraph me immediately, at my expense, if you will go or not. Do not attempt to accept my offer unless both of you are perfectly well and strong and willing to stand great hardships, for the sake of what we may have the good luck to find. And if you do go, don't blame me if we are all disappointed, and come home poorer than we went.

"If you accept the offer, I will telegraph you sufficient money to Messrs. Bartwell & Stone, Boston, to pay your fare to San Francisco, and I shall expect to see you at the latter city before the 20th of the month, for I am going to start for the new gold fields, even if I have to go with strangers, as soon as possible. With love to you both, I remain,

"Your affectionate uncle,
"FOSTER C. PORTNEY."

"Oh, Earl, let's go!" burst from Randy's lips as he finished the long letter. "This is just what I've been waiting for. Let's go to Alaska and make our fortunes!"

"Go to Alaska and be frozen to death, you mean," replied Earl; yet he smiled even as he spoke. "Do you know that the thermometer goes down to forty degrees below zero out there in winter?"

"Well, we're used to roughing it out here in these woods."

"These woods can't hold a candle to Alaska for barrenness, Randy. Think of a winter nine months long and ice all the year round! Uncle said in one of his other letters, that the ground never thawed out more than a few feet, excepting in favored localities."

"Do you mean to say you'll let such a splendid chance slip by?" demanded the younger lad, straightening up and looking his brother full in the face. "And let it slip, too, when we're in such trouble here?"

"No, I didn't say that, Randy. But we ought to consider the matter carefully before we make up our minds. According to the letter we'll have to spend at least two years in the gold fields."

"I'll spend ten if I can make money."

"Uncle said in that other letter that no one seemed to care to stay in the upper portion of Alaska more than two or three years at a time."

"Well, I'm in for the trip, heart and soul. Hurrah for the — what's the name of that creek? — Klondike! Hurrah for the Klondike! I wonder if it's on the map."

Randy rushed over to the little shelf which contained

all the school-books the family had ever possessed, and brought forth a large geography, much the worse for wear. There was no separate map of Alaska, but there was one of North America, and this he scanned with interest.

"Here's the Yukon and here's the Porcupine and the Pelly rivers, but I don't see any Klondike," he said seriously. "I wonder where it can be."

"You can't expect to find a little creek on a map that shows up the Yukon River as less than two inches long," said Earl. "Why, the Yukon is between two and three thousand miles long. Circle City must be up there," he continued, pointing to where the Yukon touched the 144° of longitude, "and if that's so, this new gold field can't be so very far off, although in such a great territory a few hundred miles this way or that are hardly counted."

"But you'll go, won't you, Earl?" pleaded Randy, as he restored the geography to the shelf. "We'll never make more than our pork and beans out here in the woods."

Earl picked up a small stick from the fireplace and brought out his pocket-knife. He always had to go to whittling when he wanted to do some hard thinking. "If we accepted Uncle Foster's invitation to come to San Francisco, there would be no turning back," he remarked, after a moment of silence.

"We shouldn't want to turn back as soon as that."

"And we couldn't turn back after we once got into Alaska. There is no such thing as travelling back and forth between the months of October and May. The rivers freeze up, and everything is snow and ice."

"Well, we'd have plenty of provisions — Uncle would be sure to see to that. We've got to vacate here, you must remember, in a day or two."

Again Earl was silent. He had sharpened up one end of the stick, and now he turned to the other. "I wonder where we could telegraph from best," he said at last.

Randy's eyes lit up instantly, and he caught his big brother by the shoulder. "Good for you, Earl; I knew you would say yes!" he cried. "Why, we can telegraph from Spruceville, can't we?"

"We can if they'll trust us for the telegram."

"If they won't, I'll pay for it. I'm not going to let such a chance slide by. The thing of it is," Randy added, sobering down suddenly, "how are we to get to Boston to get the money Uncle intends to send on?"

"We'll have to sell off our things here. They'll bring in something, although not much."

"Good! I never thought of that."

For two hours the boys talked matters over, and in the excitement dinner was entirely forgotten. Then a telegram was prepared which ran as follows: —

"Will sell out and come on as soon as possible."

It was agreed that Earl should send the message from Spruceville, a town four miles beyond Basco. This was a seven miles' tramp, but he did not mind it, having walked the distance many times previously. He procured a bite to eat, and with the letter from his uncle in his pocket he started off. He intended to show the letter to the telegraph operator in case the man should hesitate to send the message with charges to be paid at the other end.

At Basco, Earl met a number of workmen of the district, among whom was Tom Roland, the brother of the lumberman who intended to buy the timber land from Caleb Norcross. Roland was a man whom nobody liked, and Earl passed him without a word, although it was evident from Roland's manner that the latter desired to stop for a talk. With Tom Roland was a fellow named Guardley, a ne'er-do-well, who had been up before the squire on more than one occasion for drinking and stealing. The reader will do well to remember both Tom Roland and Guardley, for they are destined to play a most important part in the chapters which follow.

The middle of the afternoon had passed before Earl struck the outskirts of Spruceville and made his way to the little railroad station where was located the telegraph office. His errand was soon explained to the young man in charge, and he felt in his pocket to bring forth the slip of paper Randy had written out, and his uncle's letter.

To his consternation both were missing. He remembered well where he had placed them, yet to make sure he searched his clothing thoroughly. His search was useless. The message and the letter were gone.

CHAPTER III.

A FALSE IDENTIFICATION.

"GONE!"

That was the single word which dropped from Earl's lips as he stood at the window of the telegraph office at Spruceville and hunted for the missing letter from his Uncle Foster. He cared nothing for the message,— that could easily be rewritten,—but the letter was highly important.

Not finding it about his person, he commenced to retrace his steps with his eyes on the ground. An hour was spent in this manner, and then he returned slowly to the office.

"I want to send a message to San Francisco, and I had a letter with me to show that it was all right," he explained. "Will you send the message anyhow and collect at the other end? The man who is to receive the message wanted it sent that way."

The telegraph operator mused for a moment. Then he asked Earl who he was and where he lived, and finally said he guessed it would be all right. The message was again written out, and ten minutes later it was on its long journey westward, by way of Boston. The business finished, Earl thanked the operator and started on his return home.

He was very much out of sorts with himself, and wondered what his younger brother would think of him. "I needn't find fault with Randy for being careless after this," he sighed, almost bitterly. "I'm as bad as he is, and worse. One thing is a comfort, though: I remember the name of that Boston firm that is to provide us with our money — Bartwell & Stone. I had better make a note of that." And he did.

The evening shadows were beginning to fall when Basco was again reached. On the main street of the little town Earl halted to think matters over. Why wouldn't it be a good thing to let folks know that they wanted to sell out their household goods and their tools and other things? He made his way to the general store.

"Well, Portney, I heard you had been put off your place," was the greeting received from the general storekeeper.

"We have not been put off — we are going to leave it, Mr. Andrews."

"Oh! Where are you going?"

"To Alaska."

"Alaska? You must be joking."

"No, sir. My uncle, Foster Portney, has sent for Randy and me to come to San Francisco, and the three of us are going to some new gold fields."

"Well, what about my bill?" asked the storekeeper, anxiously. He was interested in but little outside of his business. "Of course that has got to be settled before you leave."

"We will pay up, never fear. But we want to sell off all our stuff first. Will you let me write out a notice to that effect and post it outside?"

"Yes, you can do that. Going to sell off, eh? What have you got?"

Earl enumerated the various articles he and Randy had listed to sell. They were not of great value, and the storekeeper smiled grimly.

"They won't bring much."

"They ought to bring thirty or forty dollars."

"You'll be lucky to get ten."

"Ten dollars won't see us through. We have got to get enough to pay our bills and secure our passage down to Boston."

"And how much will that be?" questioned Peleg Andrews, cautiously. Earl made a rapid calculation. With the money already on hand and that owing for tools and groceries, twenty-five dollars ought to see them through.

"We must have thirty dollars for the stuff."

Peleg Andrews said no more, but turned away to wait on a customer that had just come in. Procuring sheets of paper, Earl set to work and penned two notices, both alike, stating that the goods and chattels of the Portney brothers would be sold within the next three days, to the highest bidders, and a list of the articles followed. One of the notices was tacked up in front of the store and the other in front of the hotel, and then Earl returned home.

As the big brother had expected, Randy was much put out about the loss of the letter, but he was glad that Earl had gone ahead, nevertheless, and before he retired that night, he brought forth some of the articles to be sold, and mended and cleaned them up.

The two were eating breakfast when the first prospective buyer rode up in a farm wagon. It was a lumberman from over the ridge behind Basco, who was thinking of settling down to cabin life by himself. He made an offer of fifteen dollars for everything in sight, but Earl held out for forty dollars.

The man was about to drive away, when a second lumberman drove up, followed by Peleg Andrews in his store wagon. Both of the newcomers were eager to buy, although they affected indifference. Bidding became rather lively, and at last the goods were split up between the first comer and the storekeeper, the former paying thirty dollars and the latter twenty dollars for what they got. This made fifty dollars in all, and out of this amount Earl settled with Peleg Andrews on the spot.

It was while the men were loading the goods preparatory to taking them away, that Caleb Norcross appeared. He had expected to make a cheap purchase, and was keenly disappointed to find he was too late.

"Getting out, eh?" he ventured.

"Yes," answered Earl, briefly. "You can have your keys in a couple of hours. Here is your money."

"I ain't in any hurry," grumbled the landlord.

"Isn't Dan Roland going to take the property?" asked Randy, curiously.

"No, he backed out last night," answered Caleb Norcross, and to avoid being questioned further he moved away.

Fortunately for the two boys, there was an old trunk in the cabin, and also a small wooden box which could be made to hold clothing, and these they packed with such effects as they intended to take along. A bargain was struck with the man who had failed to purchase any of the other goods, and the two boxes were placed in his wagon, and then the lads were ready to leave the spot which had been their home for many years.

"Well, I'm sure I wish you success," said Peleg Andrews, as he shook each by the hand. "But it looks foolhardy to me — going away off to Alaska."

"You'll be glad enough to come back home, see if you don't," put in Caleb Norcross. He did not offer to shake hands, at which the boys were just as well satisfied. In a minute more the brothers were up beside the lumberman on the wagon seat, the whip cracked, and the horse started; and the long trip to Alaska could be said to have fairly begun.

A stop was made at Basco, where Earl settled up such bills as still remained unpaid, and then the horse set off on a trot for Spruceville, which was reached less than three-quarters of an hour later. At the latter place a way train for Bangor was due, and they had barely time to procure tickets and get their baggage checked before it came along and took them on board.

"We've made a flying start and no mistake," was Randy's comment, as he leaned back in the cushioned seat. "Two days ago we never dreamed of going to Alaska or anywhere else."

"I hope we haven't any cause to regret our hasty action," answered Earl, gravely. Then he immediately brightened up. "But we've started now, so let us make the most of it."

The ride over the rough roads had made them hungry, but they had to wait until Bangor was reached before they could obtain anything to eat. It was late in the evening when the train rolled into the station and they alighted. Both boys had been in Bangor several times, so they did not feel quite like strangers. Having obtained supper at a restaurant, they made their way to the river docks and asked concerning the boat for Boston, having decided to make that trip by water. The boat was in, and having procured their passage, they were privileged to go on board and sleep there overnight.

The trip to Boston was an uneventful one, although full of novelty to Earl and Randy, who had never taken such a voyage before. They might have enjoyed it still more had they not been so anxious concerning what was before them. Alas! little did they dream of all the grave perils the future held in store.

"We don't want to look too green," said Earl, when the steamboat was tying up at her wharf and the passengers were preparing to go ashore.

"Oh, I guess we'll pass in a crowd," said Randy, laughing. "All we want to look out for is that we are not robbed, or something like that."

Leaving their baggage on check, the two boys started from Foster's wharf up into the city. They had no idea where the firm of Bartwell & Stone were located, but Earl was certain they could easily be found by consulting a directory.

The elder brother was on the point of entering a large store in quest of the book mentioned when Randy pulled his arm and pointed down the street. "There goes a fire engine, Earl!" he cried. "Let's follow it. I should like to see how they manage a fire in a city."

Earl was willing, and away they went, easily keeping up with the engine, which had to proceed slowly through the crowded thoroughfare. The fire was in a paint and oil works, and burnt fiercely for over an hour before it was gotten under control. The boys lingered around, watching the movements of the firemen with keen interest, and it was two hours later before Earl caught Randy by the shoulder and hauled him out of the mob of people.

"Remember, we're bound for Alaska," he said. "We can't afford to stop at every sight on the way."

A few blocks further on a directory was found in a drug store and the address of Bartwell & Stone jotted down. They lost no further time in hunting up the firm of bankers and brokers, who occupied the ground floor of a substantial business structure.

"I am Earl Portney," explained Earl, to the clerk who asked them what they wanted. "This is my brother Randolph. Our uncle, Foster Portney, said he would send on some money for us from San Francisco. Has it arrived yet?"

"I'll see. Was it a telegraph order?"

"I suppose so."

The clerk disappeared into an inner apartment, to be gone several minutes. When he came out he was accompanied by a tall, sharp-eyed man in rusty black.

"These are not the young men who called for the money," said the man in rusty black. "There must be some mistake here."

"Were the other men identified, Mr. Stone?" questioned the clerk, while both Randy and Earl pricked up their ears.

"Oh, yes; a clerk from Johnston's restaurant identified them as Earl and Randolph Portney. Besides, they held the original letter which had been sent by their uncle, Foster Portney, from San Francisco."

CHAPTER IV.

A SERIOUS SET-BACK.

EARL and Randy could scarcely believe their ears. What was this gentleman in rusty black saying, that two men had been identified as themselves and had called for the money sent on by their Uncle Foster?

"There is a mistake somewhere," said the clerk, turning to the brothers. "You say you are Earl and Randolph Portney?"

"We are," both replied, in a breath.

"Two men were here not two hours ago and were identified as the ones to receive the money. They had a letter from their uncle, in which he wanted them to come to San Francisco and join him in a trip to Alaska."

"That letter was ours!" burst out Earl. "I lost it a couple of days ago."

The clerk turned to the elderly gentleman, who looked more serious than ever.

"Have you any idea who those men were?" asked the gentleman.

"They were a couple of thieves, that's certain," said

Randy, bluntly. "The money was to come to us and nobody else."

"Where did you lose that letter?"

"I lost it on the road between Naddy Brook and Spruceville," replied Earl, and gave some of the particulars. The full story of his uncle's offer to Randy and himself followed, to which Mr. Stone listened closely. He was a fair judge of human nature, and saw at once that the two boys were no sharpers and that their story was most likely true.

"Well, if you are the real Portney brothers, we are out exactly three hundred dollars," he said, after considerable talking. "I paid over that money in good faith, too, on the strength of the letter and the identification."

"We had nothing to do with that," answered Earl, stoutly, feeling he must stand up for his rights.

"Of course not, but — Just wait here a few minutes, and I'll try to find that clerk from the restaurant who identified the rascals."

Mr. Stone put on a silk hat and went out, to be gone nearly or quite half an hour. He returned accompanied by another man — a police official — to whom the particulars of the occurrence had been given.

"That identification was also part of the swindle," the broker explained. "I could not find the clerk at the restaurant, and I am convinced now that he was not the man he made me believe he was."

"But what about our money?" said Earl, coldly, thinking the broker might try to shift the responsibility of the affair.

"If you can find some reliable party known to us to identify you, I will pay the sum to you," was the answer. "But I've got to be sure of the identification this time — and you can't blame me for that," added the broker, with a short laugh.

"No, we can't blame you for that," repeated Earl, yet at the same time wondering who there was in that strange city who knew them.

"I don't know of any one here who knows us," put in Randy, reading his elder brother's thought. "I wish Uncle had sent the money in some other way."

"See here," put in the police official. "Since those swindlers had the letter that was lost up near where you come from, perhaps you know the men. Mr. Stone, can't you describe them?"

As well as he was able the broker did so. But the description was so indefinite that both Earl and Randy shook their heads.

"I know a dozen men who look a good deal like that description," said the older brother. "It's possible they were lumbermen like ourselves."

"Yes, they did look like lumbermen," replied Mr. Stone. "That is why I was not so particular about their identification."

For another half hour the matter was talked over.

and then as it was getting time to close up the office for the day, Earl and Randy left, to find some one to identify them, were such a thing possible. At the corner of the block both halted.

"I'm blessed if I know what to do," were Randy's words. "I can't think of a soul who knows us here."

"There used to be a man named Curtis Gordon who once lived at Basco — he owned the feed mill there. He came to Boston and started a flour business. But whether he would remember me is a question. He hasn't seen me in about eight years."

"We might try him — it would be better than nothing!" cried Randy, eagerly. "Let us hunt him up in the directory."

This was done, and they found Mr. Curtis Gordon's place of business after a search lasting over an hour. Several clerks were in attendance who supplied the information that Mr. Gordon had gone to New York, and would not be back for two days.

"Stumped again," murmured Randy, dismally. "Did you ever see such luck!"

"Never give up," answered Earl, as cheerfully as he could. "I wonder if Mrs. Gordon lives in town."

"What if she does?"

"I'd call on her, and perhaps she can help us out. She used to know me."

From the clerks in the store they received the Gordons' home address. It was a fine place on the Back Bay, and it was nightfall by the time the boys reached it. They were ushered into the waiting-hall by a servant, who immediately went off to notify her mistress, who was at dinner.

From the dining-room came a murmur of talking, and one of the voices sounded strangely familiar to Earl. "Hark, Randy," he whispered. "Isn't that Squire Dobson speaking?"

"It is!" ejaculated Randy. "We are saved at last!"

Mrs. Gordon came to them a minute later, having excused herself to her guest. The boys' mission was soon explained, Earl at the same time offering an excuse for calling at the meal hour. He mentioned Squire Dobson, and that individual was called from the table.

"Well, well!" exclaimed the squire of Basco, a short, stout, and rather jolly type of a country official. "I didn't expect to see you in Boston, although I heard yesterday that you were bound for Alaska or some such place. Mrs. Gordon, these are Daniel Portney's boys,— you must remember Daniel Portney,— the one who lost his life in that dreadful forest fire up our way some years ago."

Mrs. Gordon did remember, and she gave both lads a warm greeting. It was several minutes before Earl could get down to business, and then the matter of identification was left to Squire Dobson, who said he would see them through in the morning, as soon as the Bartwell & Stone offices were open.

"I don't know them," he said, "but I know some bankers on the same block, and we can introduce each other."

Mrs. Gordon was glad enough to see some folks from the district which had once been her home, and asked the brothers to partake of dinner with the squire and her family of boys and girls. After some hesitation, the invitation was accepted, and two hours were spent at the mansion.

During the course of this time it was learned by Earl and Randy that Squire Dobson had come down from Maine in search of his son, a happy-go-lucky lad, who had run away from home, as previously mentioned. The squire had heard from a friend that Fred had been seen near the docks in Boston, but he had been unable so far to locate the wayward youth.

"I'm afraid he has either gone to New York or on some long ocean trip," said the squire to Earl. "He's a foolish boy and is causing me no end of trouble. If you ever run across him, send him home at once."

"I will — if he'll go," answered Earl; but neither he nor Randy ever dreamed of meeting Fred Dobson where they did.

The visit over, the brothers left, to hunt up some cheap hotel at which to stop for the night. This was an easy matter, and at ten o'clock they retired. A sound sleep, however, was out of the question, for both were anxious concerning the outcome of their dealings with Bartwell & Stone.

Promptly at the hour appointed they met the squire at the office of the brokers and bankers. Another banker, well known to both Squire Dobson and to Mr. Stone, was introduced all around, and thus Randy and Earl's identification was established beyond a doubt. This accomplished, Earl received three hundred dollars in cash, for which he and Randy signed a receipt; and the transaction was over.

Just outside of the office, the boys separated from the squire of Basco, and the former lost no time in making their way to the depot of the New York & New England Railroad.

"I don't know what route is best to take to San Francisco," said Earl. "I guess we had better buy tickets as far as New York first." And this was done; and a few hours later saw them safe on board a train, with their baggage in the car ahead. At the depot Earl had obtained a number of folders of different routes to the west, and these he intended to study while on his way to the great metropolis.

"Oh, but railroad travelling is fine!" cried Randy, enthusiastically, as the long train sped on its way through hills and valleys, and past numerous pretty towns and villages, all alive with the hum of a thousand industries. "One feels as if he would like to ride forever!"

"I'm afraid you'll be tired of riding by the time we reach San Francisco," said Earl, who, nevertheless, also enjoyed the journey. "This is only a little trip of six or seven hours. The next will be one of many days and nights."

"I wonder how they sleep on a train," went on Randy, curiously.

"We'll learn soon enough, Randy. Only don't let every one see how green we are," added Earl, in a whisper.

At one of the stations in Connecticut, where a ten minutes' stop was made, the two lads alighted to stretch their legs and take a look around. They had been seated in the last car, and now they walked forward along the broad platform.

Suddenly Randy caught his brother's arm. "Earl! Earl! look!" he ejaculated, and pointed to a window of the smoking-car. "There are Tom Roland and Jasper Guardley! What can they be doing on this train?"

Earl glanced to where Randy pointed and saw that his brother was right. At the same instant Tom Roland saw them, and he drew back and motioned for his companion to do the same. Earl noted the movement and stood stock-still.

"Randy, I wonder —" he began, and stopped short.

"What, Earl? Isn't it queer they should be on this train from Boston?"

"Yes. Randy, do you think it is possible that Tom Roland would be so dishonest as to — to — "

"To get that money, Earl?" broke in the younger boy. "He might be — and yes, Mr. Stone's description of the two swindlers fits Roland and Guardley exactly!"

CHAPTER V.

A NIGHT IN NEW YORK.

"The description certainly does fit these two men," said Earl, with some hesitation. "And it is queer that Roland should be down here, when only a few days ago he was in Basco. Guardley, I know, is not above cheating — he's been up before Squire Dobson several times for it."

"Let us go and have a talk with them," said Randy, impulsively. "If they stole that money, I want to know it."

"It's not our business to hunt those swindlers up," answered Earl, hesitatingly; yet he followed Randy to the platform of the smoking-car, and they were soon inside, and making their way to where Roland and Guardley sat, pulling away at two black-looking cigars.

"How do you do, Earl?" said Tom Roland, familiarly, as soon as the boys appeared. "It's queer we should be on the same train, isn't it?"

"It is queer," answered Earl, stiffly, taken aback by the greeting. "Where are you bound?"

"Guardley and I are going to try our luck in the West. Say, I heard you boys were bound for Alaska. Is that true?"

"Yes."

"It costs a heap to go there — didn't know you had so much money," put in Guardley, with a smile that neither Earl nor Randy appreciated.

"And I didn't know you had any money for a Western trip," returned the older brother, rather sharply.

"Oh, Tom here is seeing me through," answered Guardley; but both Randy and Earl noted that he appeared somewhat confused for the moment.

"Guardley has done me several good turns, and it wouldn't be fair for me to turn my back on him," finished Tom Roland. "We are going right through to San Francisco. How about yourselves?"

"We stop off at New York," said Randy.

"It's a pity we can't travel together—" began Roland, when Earl cut him short.

"Roland, did you pick up a letter belonging to me?" asked the boy.

The man's eyes dropped, but only for the fraction of a second. "A letter belonging to you?" he repeated. "No. Where did you lose it?"

"Somewhere around Basco. Did you see it, Guardley?"

The second man shook his head. "Was it important?" he asked.

"Very," said Earl, laconically, and then, as the train began to move again he motioned to Randy, and the two started back for their seat in the last car.

"What do you think?" questioned Randy, when they were seated.

"I don't know what to think. It's mighty queer the pair should leave Basco in such a hurry."

"We left in a hurry. But we had a good reason."

"And they may have — a reason most folks don't look for."

"Do you think they left on account of some crooked work?" cried Randy.

"That would probably be Jasper Guardley's reason for getting away. But it's not our affair, and we have enough other matters to think of," concluded Earl, after a pause. "When we get to New York we'll be like stray cattle in a hundred-acre lot. We must look out not to get lost, and above all things not to lose our money."

"And engage the cheapest and quickest passage to San Francisco," said Randy. "Let us look over those folders before it gets too late. It's too dark to see much outside."

The lamps were lighted in the car, and they lost no further time in digesting the contents of the folders of the railroad companies and pouring over the maps of the various routes to the Golden Gate.

"One looks about as good as another on paper,"

remarked Earl, at last. "I think we had best take the New York Central Railroad to Chicago, then the Rock Island & Chicago to Rock Island, and then the Southern Pacific. We'll find out about that route when we reach New York."

It was exactly ten o'clock in the evening that the train rolled into the Grand Central Depot at Forty-second Street and Randy and Earl alighted. The crowd was very thick, and though both looked for Roland and Guardley, the two men could not be discovered. The coming and going of so many people confused them, and the many cries which greeted them as they emerged on the street did not tend to set them at ease.

"Cab, sir? Coupé? This way for the Broadway Central Hotel! Evening papers, *Post* or *Telegram! Mail and Express!*"

Several came up to the two boys, offering them cab rides and the like, but both Randy and Earl shook their heads. Then Earl remembered that the ticket office was close at hand, and he and his brother went inside again. A long talk with the ticket clerk followed, and they concluded to take the New York Central road to Chicago, and from there as previously intended. The train would start at ten in the morning, and Earl bought two tickets, paying an amount which brought their cash balance down quite low once more.

"Never mind; that pays for about all we'll need," said Randy. "Let us leave the tickets to be called for, and then they'll be safe."

"No indeed!" said Earl. "Some one may call for them just as the money was called for. I'll carry my ticket in an inside pocket, and you had best do the same."

This settled, the brothers strolled out once more. It was rather late, but they could not resist the temptation to a walk down Broadway, of which they had heard so often. They trudged as far as the Post-office, took a look at Park Row and the numerous newspaper buildings, and the Brooklyn Bridge all lit up in a blaze of electric lights, and then Earl happened to glance at the clock on St. Paul's Church.

"Half-past twelve, Randy!" he ejaculated. "Gracious! we'll never find a hotel open as late as this! Let us get back to the vicinity of the depot again!"

"I guess the hotels are open all night here," answered the younger brother. "Let us ride up Broadway on that street car." And they boarded a cable car, which speedily took them back to Forty-second Street. A convenient hotel was found close to the railroad station, and they lost no time in retiring. The constant rumble and roar of the elevated trains disturbed them not a little, and it was well into the morning hours before both dropped off into dreamland, not to awaken until a bell boy aroused **them** at seven o'clock.

After a hasty breakfast another look was taken around the city. Finding they had the time, they took an elevated train to the Battery and back, staying long enough at the lower end of the city to catch a glimpse of Castle Garden with its aquarium, and the statue of Liberty out in the bay.

"One could spend a month in sight-seeing here," sighed Randy. "I wish we had had the time to do Boston and New York thoroughly."

Ten o'clock found them on the train which was to take them through to Chicago without change of cars. The cars were comfortably filled, but there was no crowding. Again they looked for Roland and Guardley, but without success.

"I guess they remained in New York," said Earl; but for once the young fellow was mistaken.

Leaving the vicinity of the metropolis, the train began its long journey up the beautiful Hudson. But the journey northward did not last long. Soon the train branched to the westward and plunged into the hills and rolling lands of the Mohawk Valley. City after city were left behind with a whir and a rush that almost took Randy's breath from him. At noon a stop was made for lunch, then on they went again. Supper was served in a dining-car, and both boys voted it about the best meal they had ever tasted.

After the lamps were lit it was not long before the passengers began to think of going to bed. Both

Randy and Earl watched the porter closely as he drew out the beds from the narrow closets in the sloping roof of the car, set up the little wooden partitions, and otherwise arranged the sleeping-apartments. The boys had a section to themselves and concluded to sleep together in the lower berth, so the upper berth was left out.

"A sleeping-car is a great institution," said Earl, as they turned in. "Why, a train like this is just a moving house and nothing else!"

Shortly after noon of the day following Chicago was reached. Here they had a three hours' stop and spent the time in a ride on State Street, and a trip to the roof of the great Masonic Temple, where a grand bird's-eye view of the entire city was to be seen, spread out far below them.

And so the long trip westward continued. To tell of all the places stopped at would be impossible. All day long for nearly a week they sat at their car window taking in the sights of cities, towns, prairies, and mountains. There were wonderful bridges to cross and perilous turns to make, at which both held their breath, expecting each moment to be dashed to pieces. In the mountains a severe storm was encountered, and the rolling of the thunder was awe-inspiring, so long was it kept up.

But all journeys, long and short, must come to an end, and one fine morning the boys found themselves safe and sound in San Francisco, and on their way to the

Palace Hotel. The trip overland had brightened them a good bit, and they no longer looked as green as when they had started.

They had just stepped from a Market Street car in front of the hotel when they saw a youth coming down the hotel steps who looked strangely familiar, in spite of the somewhat ragged clothing he wore.

"Randy, who is that fellow?" questioned Earl, quickly, as he caught his brother by the elbow.

"Why, if it isn't Fred Dobson!" burst from Randy's lips. "How in the world did he get away out here? Fred Dobson! Fred Dobson! Stop, we want to talk to you!" he called out, as the youth in question was on the point of hurrying off.

CHAPTER VI.

PREPARATIONS FOR DEPARTURE.

"RANDY PORTNEY!" came from the lips of the boy addressed, as he turned to stare at the person who had called out his name. "And Earl, too! Where — where did you come from?"

"From Basco, of course," returned Randy. "How did you get away out here?"

"I — I came out on a train from Chicago," stammered Fred Dobson, but he did not add that the train had been a freight, and that the stolen ride had been both uncomfortable and full of peril.

"We met your father in Boston," put in Earl. "He said if we should ever run across you to tell you to come home."

"I'm not going back," was the reply of the squire's son. "I came out here to make my fortune."

"I'm afraid you'll find it rather hard work," ventured Randy, and he glanced at Fred's shabby suit. Around Basco the youth had dressed better than any one else.

"I've been playing in hard luck lately," was the

slangy reply. "But say, what are you two fellows doing out here?"

"We came on to join our uncle," said Randy. "He is going to take us to Alaska with him."

"Alaska! To those new gold fields a fellow reads about in the daily papers?"

"Yes."

"I'd like to go there myself," said the runaway, readily.

"It costs a good deal of money to go, Fred," remarked Earl. He rather liked the squire's son, in spite of his wild ways. "A fellow must take along a year's provisions."

"So I've heard. I wonder if I couldn't work my way up on one of the boats."

"I wouldn't advise you to go," said Randy. "Why, you are not used to hard work, and they say work up there is of the hardest kind."

"Oh, I can work if I have to. Where is your uncle?"

"He's stopping at this hotel." Randy turned to Earl. "Let us see if Uncle Foster is in, and we can talk to Fred some time later."

This was decided upon, and the squire's son walked off, promising to be back in a few hours.

"He puts on a pretty good face, but I fancy he is homesick, nevertheless," remarked Earl, as he and Randy made their way to the hotel office. They were just about to ask for their uncle when a hand was laid on Earl's shoulder.

"Earl! Randy! How are you, my boys! Just as fresh and hearty as when I saw you last. And how both of you are growing! Why, Earl, you are almost a man! I'm glad to see you, yes, I am!" And Foster Portney beamed at both from a pair of brown eyes set in a round, ruddy face, which was half covered with a long beard. He was a large and rugged man, and his open manner had made him many friends.

"What a beard you've got, Uncle Foster!" were Randy's first words, as he winced at the close grip Foster Portney gave his hand. "You look like all the rest of the Westerners around here!"

"I'm glad we had no trouble in finding you," put in Earl, whose hand also tingled from the grip given it. He remembered now that his uncle had always been considered an unusually strong man. "I know he'll stand the Alaskan climate well enough, even if we don't," he thought.

"Didn't have any trouble getting here, did you?" questioned Foster Portney. "Your message came on time?"

"We had a little set-back in Boston," answered Earl, and told of the trouble about the money. His uncle listened with a sober look on his broad face.

"That was too bad, truly, lads. But it's the loss of that firm of bankers and brokers. They ought to have been sure of the identification. And you think the thieves were two men named Roland and Guardley? They must be thorough rascals."

"We are not sure," broke in Randy, hastily. "It only looks that way."

"I see." Foster Portney mused for a moment. "Well, we can't lose time in trying to investigate. I was hoping you two boys would turn up to-day or to-morrow. Day after to-morrow a boat sails for Juneau, and if I rustle around I think I can secure passage for ourselves and our traps. If we don't catch this boat, we'll have to wait two weeks, or else take a train for Portland and wait ten days."

"But we haven't a thing, Uncle Foster," cried Randy. "That is, outside of our clothing, which is in our trunks, on check at the railroad station."

"And that clothing, for the most part, will have to be left behind, Randy. For a country like Alaska one must be differently dressed than here. Each of you will have to have a suit of furs and plenty of flannels and all that sort of thing."

"And where shall we get them?"

"There is a regular outfitting store not far from here. But the first thing to be done, now you have turned up, is to secure those passage tickets to Juneau. The Alaskan fever is setting in strong here, and we'll not be alone on our trip over Chilkoot Pass and along the headwaters of the Yukon."

"I'm in the dark about this trip, I must confess," said Earl. "Where is this pass you mention, and where is the Klondike Creek, or River?"

"I'll show you the route to-night, boys, on a map just issued by our government, the best map out so far. But come along to that steamboat office, or we'll get left."

Five minutes later saw the boys and their uncle on a street car which ran close to the dock at which the steamboat lay, taking in her cargo, which consisted mainly of the outfits of miners and prospectors. The boat, which was named the *Golden Hope*, had been chartered especially for this trip, and a temporary shipping office had been established close at hand. Around this office was congregated a motley collection of men, all eager to obtain passage to Juneau as cheaply as it could be had.

Through this crowd Foster Portney shoved his way, with Randy and Earl close behind him. It was some minutes before they could get to the ticket office.

"I want three tickets," said Mr. Portney. "How much freight will you carry on them?"

"Six hundred pounds, and not a pound more for anybody," was the quick reply.

"And when do you sail?"

"Wednesday, at twelve o'clock sharp. What are the names? We don't want any mix-up in this rush."

The names were put down, and the money for the passage paid over, and with their tickets in their pockets the three struggled to get out of the crowd, which was growing more dense every minute. Close at hand was a big bill-board on which was posted a large circular headed in big black letters: —

THE GOLD FIELDS OF ALASKA!
Direct Route via Juneau and Over Chilkoot Pass!
Now is the Time to Go and Stake Your Claim!

"That circular is enough to set almost any one crazy." said Earl, as he read it over. "Well, I hope we strike a bonanza."

"The reports are very encouraging," replied Foster Portney, who, in spite of his usual cool headedness had the gold fever nearly as badly as any one in San Francisco. "You see," he went on, "the sooner we get there the better; for we won't have much time left after arriving before the long and terribly cold winter sets in."

Earl had imagined that the six hundred pounds of freight must be divided between the three, but soon learned that six hundred pounds was the limit for each person.

"We'll never carry that much, will we?" he queried. "Why, how are we going to get all that stuff over the pass you mentioned?"

"We'll get Indians to pack it over. They'll charge twenty or thirty cents a pound, but it's the best that can be done. Some hire pack mules and dog teams, but my experience has been that Indians are the most reliable."

Dinner was now had, and then the three proceeded to the outfitting store Foster Portney had previously mentioned. On the way their uncle asked the boys what they had in their trunks, that nothing not needed might be purchased.

Two hours were spent in buying clothing, and both Earl and Randy thought their uncle would never get done adding to the pile. First came a dozen suits of flannel underwear, and with them a dozen pairs of heavy socks and half a dozen of light ones. Then came two suits of woollen clothing, strongly made and with large pockets, two pairs of strong shoes and a pair of arctics, and two pairs of walrus-hide boots — heavy, it is true, but strong as iron. Finally came a suit of furs and two caps, each with a guard which could be pulled down to the neck, leaving only two holes for the eyes.

"I reckon you've got handkerchiefs and such extras." said Mr. Portney. "So now all you want, so far as wearing is concerned, is a few pairs of smoked glasses, to prevent snow-blindness."

The general outfitter was also able to supply these, and he suggested they take along about ten yards of mosquito netting.

"Mosquito netting!" cried Randy. "What for?"

"During the short summer mosquitoes are exceedingly thick in Alaska," said his uncle; and made the purchase suggested.

It was now getting late, and Foster Portney said they

had best wait until the following morning before buying the camping-out things, bedding, and other necessities. "I'll make a careful list to-night," he added.

They returned to the Palace Hotel, where Randy and Earl found Fred Dobson awaiting them.

"Say!" was the greeting of the squire's son. "Is half of Basco moving out to San Francisco?"

"What do you mean?" questioned Earl, with a puzzled look.

"Why, I was down at the railroad station about an hour ago, and I saw a train come in from Chicago with Tom Roland and Jasper Guardley on board."

CHAPTER VII.

BUYING THE OUTFITS.

"You saw Tom Roland and Jasper Guardley?" burst from the lips of the Portney brothers simultaneously.

"Yes," replied Fred Dobson. "I couldn't believe my eyes at first, but when I felt sure I was right I ran up to speak to Roland."

"And what did he say?" queried Earl.

"He didn't give me a chance to speak to him. He and Guardley disappeared in the crowd like a flash. I rather think they saw me and avoided me."

Earl and Randy exchanged glances. Tom Roland and Jasper Guardley had followed them to San Francisco. What could it mean?

"I shouldn't wonder if they are bound for Alaska, too!" burst out Randy. "Oh, Earl, supposing they got that letter—"

"It's more than likely they did," said the elder youth, quickly. I'll wager both of them are going to try their fortunes in the new gold fields. Well, they had a cheap trip West," he concluded bitterly.

"If we could prove they got the money, we could have them locked up."

"But we can't prove it, Randy; we haven't time, so we'll just have to let matters stand where they are. For my part I never want to see either of them again," said Earl, decidedly.

Fred Dobson had listened to the latter part of the conversation with interest, and now he wished to know what it all meant.

"They must be guilty," he said, after Randy had recited the facts. "Guardley is a bad egg. You know he was up before my father several times. But say, Randy," he went on, as Earl turned away with Foster Portney to secure extra accommodations at the hotel for the two following nights, "can't you fix it up with your uncle so that I can go to Alaska with him? I'll work like a slave for the chance to go."

Randy had expected something of this sort and had talked the matter over with Earl, and now he shook his head.

"I don't believe I can, Fred. My uncle is only taking us along because we are related and because he knows we are both strong and used to hard work. I really don't believe you could stand it in the new gold fields. He has warned us that the exposure is something awful."

"Oh, I know, but I can stand more than you think," pleaded Fred.

"Besides that, it wouldn't be right," added Randy. "You ran away from home, and it's your duty to go back."

"Oh, don't preach. My father doesn't care where I am."

"Yes, he does, Fred; he cares a good deal. And then your mother must be worried, too."

At the mention of his mother, Fred Dobson's face changed color for a moment, and when next he spoke there seemed to be a suspicious lump in his throat.

"I — I'm going to send mother a letter; I'll write it to-night."

"You should have written long ago, Fred."

"Oh, don't preach. Then you won't speak to your uncle?" And the squire's son looked into Randy's face wistfully.

"Yes, I'll speak to him; but it won't do any good, Fred."

It was not long after this that Foster Portney and Earl came back, having hired an extra room for the time desired. The uncle had been introduced to Fred, and now he invited the runaway to take supper with them.

It was not until the meal was nearly over that Fred urged Randy to broach the subject next his heart. Foster Portney listened patiently to all Randy had to say and also gave ear to Fred's pleadings. But his face did not brighten up into anything like an encouraging look.

"No, Dobson, I can't take you," was his reply. "In the first place, Earl and Randy are all the companions I wish to take along, that is, and grub stake, as we term it in mining slang — pay their way, that means; and in the second place, it wouldn't be right. You are a minor and have run away from home, and, if anything, it is my duty to see that you go back. Besides this, you do not look strong, and, I believe, you have never done any real hard work, and that won't do for Alaska. Only those who know how to rough it stand any show whatever of getting along there. My advice to you is, to go back where you belong."

As may be surmised, this plain speech did not suit Fred Dobson at all, and he felt more than ill at ease for the remainder of the repast. As soon as he could do so gracefully he arose to go.

"I don't suppose I'll see you again for a long while," he said, as he held out his hand to Earl and to Randy. "Well, good luck to you, anyway."

Randy caught Earl by the arm and gave it a little pinch. "How are you off for cash, Fred?" he asked, in a low tone.

"Oh, I've got a little money with me," answered Fred, quietly, but did not add that the sum-total of his fortune amounted to exactly sixty-five cents.

"Perhaps we can help you a little," put in Earl,

who understood the pinch Randy had given him. "We haven't much, but if a few dollars will do any good—"

"Will you let me have two dollars?" asked the squire's son, eagerly.

"Yes."

"And I'll let you have two more," added Randy, and the amounts were passed over on the spot, and Fred thanked them very profusely. A few minutes later he had thanked Foster Portney for the supper, bade all good-by, and was gone.

"Not a half bad boy," was the comment of Mr. Portney. "His one fault is, I reckon, that he has been allowed to have his own way too long. Roughing it out here will most likely make a man of him, unless he gets into bad company and goes to the dogs."

"I am going to write to his folks and let them know where he is," said Earl; and the letter was penned and mailed before he went to bed.

The three were on their way early on the following morning to complete the purchase of their outfits, for all must be packed up and on the steamboat deck by seven o'clock the next morning, to insure being stored on board of the *Golden Hope*.

The first purchases made were those of a good tent, bedding, woollen blankets, rubber sleeping-bags, a large piece of oiled canvas, and several lynx-skin robes.

"Now for our tools with which to cut down trees,

build boats, and the like," said Foster Portney. "Remember, we are almost like pioneers in a new land."

For boat-building purposes they purchased a good whip-saw, a cross-cut saw, a jack plane, and a draw knife, a large and a small axe, a hammer, brace and bits, six pounds of assorted nails, several pounds of oakum for calking, and some pitch. To this outfit was added fifty yards of three-quarter-inch rope.

"Don't we want some canvas for sail?" asked Randy, who was intensely interested, and who felt somewhat as if he was going out to play at Robinson Crusoe.

"No, the other bits of canvas will do for that," responded Foster Portney. "Now for the camping-out things," he went on, and had soon procured a good-sized water kettle, a frying-pan, broiler, bean pot, tin measure, extra baking and cooking tins, three tin plates and cups, three sets of knives and forks, coffee pot and strainer, salt and pepper shakers, and a strong paper-fibre water pail.

"That about ends that," he said, when each article bought had been carefully scrutinized to see that it was perfect. "Now for food and medicines, and then we'll be about done."

The food list made Randy smile grimly. "No luxuries there," he whispered to Earl. "We are going to live as plain as we did up in Maine, or plainer."

The list consisted of the following: A hundred pounds of flour, with baking-powder, twenty pounds of smoked ham and bacon, two dozen cans of tomatoes, a dozen cans of other vegetables, a small sack of potatoes, a dozen cans of condensed milk, twenty pounds of sugar, ten pounds of salt, twenty pounds of coffee, a sack of beans, pepper and other spices, and mustard. To these were added a few cans of fruit by way of delicacies.

The food packed, they made their way to a drug store and procured a small family chest of various medicines, and added to this several bottles of liquor, which, however, were to be used only for medicinal purposes, for none of the party were drinkers.

Foster Portney already had a serviceable pistol, and he now procured for this weapon a sufficient supply of cartridges. He also bought a pistol for Randy and a shot-gun for Earl. "The gun will be the most useful weapon," he said, "for it will help put lots of game into our eating-pot, and that is what we shall want."

"Won't we want a fishing-line or two?" asked Earl. "I have one in my trunk, but it is not of much account."

"Yes, we'll buy several first-class ones, and a book of flies. Fish to a hungry man are as acceptable as any other game," answered his uncle, and the articles mentioned were purchased without delay.

The list was now filled, yet Foster Portney spent nearly an hour more in picking up such odds and ends as pins, needles, spools of thread, three good pocket compasses, and burning-glasses, a pocket notebook for each, with pencils and some writing-paper and envelopes. Finally he took them to a little shop on a side street, where each procured a monstrous knapsack of oiled canvas, having straps to be placed over the shoulders and an extra strap to come up over the front part of the head.

"What an affair!" said Randy, with a laugh. "I never saw a knapsack with a head-piece before."

"You'll find it an easy thing to carry," said his uncle. "Try it," and Randy did so, and was astonished to learn how much the head-strap improved the carrying powers.

The best part of the evening was spent in packing the things they had purchased, and it was not until after ten o'clock that the last of the bundles were ready and duly tagged.

"Now we have only a few more things to get," said Foster Portney, "the most important of the whole outfit;" and as Randy and Earl looked at him blankly, he smiled in an odd way. "What could three gold hunters do without picks, shovels, and pans?"

"To be sure!" shouted Randy, and Earl reddened over the idea that he had not thought of the things before.

"We'll get them in the morning, for they won't have to be packed," said the uncle. "We have done enough for to-day."

And Randy, who was tired out, agreed with him that it had been a busy day, indeed. He went to bed with his head in a whirl about Alaska and how they were to get there, and of the wonderful finds of gold which awaited all hands. He was full of the brightest of hopes, and the hardships so soon to be encountered did not bother him.

CHAPTER VIII.

ON THE WAY TO JUNEAU.

"GET up, Randy! Don't you know we are to start for Alaska to-day?" cried Earl, at six o'clock on the following morning. "Come now, turn out."

"Oh my, but I'm tired still!" grumbled Randy, as he stretched himself. Nevertheless, he hopped out of bed a moment later and was dressed almost as soon as his brother. They had barely finished when their uncle came to summon them to breakfast.

"We'll hunt up those tools and then I have a little private business to attend to," announced Foster Portney. "So we must move lively."

Breakfast, the last meal to be eaten in San Francisco, was quickly disposed of, and then followed a half-hour's inspection of various picks, shovels, and gold-washing pans at a hardware store that made a specialty of miners' tools. The boys were greatly interested, and, as Earl said, it made them feel more like prospectors to own a pick and a shovel each. The final bundle was made and shipped to the steamboat dock, and Foster Portney left them.

"Meet me at the dock at eleven o'clock," he said, as he hurried away.

The boys had still several private matters to be settled. Their trunks were to be sold, also some old clothing. At the hotel they obtained the addresses of several dealers in second-hand goods, and they had one of the dealers call and look at the stuff. He offered ten dollars for the lot; and, as they did not see their way to doing better, they accepted his terms, and the goods were removed without delay.

"Let us take a walk around while we have the chance," said Earl. "It is only ten o'clock."

Randy was willing, and off they started up Market Street to the City Hall, and then back and into Montgomery and Kearney streets, taking in all the sights as they went. Almost before they knew it, it was time to go to the wharf.

"We don't want to keep Uncle Foster waiting," said Earl; but when they reached the wharf their uncle was nowhere in sight.

The crowd which had collected to see the gold seekers off was a large one, and more people kept coming every moment. The almost magic name, Klondike, was on every tongue, and there were hundreds who expressed the wish that they were going along.

"Alaska is full of gold!" one man declared. "Full of gold! All you've got to do is to locate it."

"That's just it," said Earl to his brother. "If you can locate it you're all right; if not—" and he finished by a shrug of his broad shoulders.

"You're not sorry we're going, are you?" demanded Randy, quickly.

"Sorry? Not a bit of it. But it doesn't pay to be too sanguine, Randy, my boy."

Quarter of an hour passed, and the jam on the dock began to become uncomfortable. Brawny men predominated, but there were also many others there,—wives to bid good-by to their husbands, girls to wish their lovers good-luck, and children to catch a last embrace from their parents. Many of the women were in tears, and a number of other eyes were moist, and altogether the scene was rather a sober one.

"What can be keeping Uncle Foster?" asked Randy, as the minutes to the time for sailing slipped by. "I don't see him anywhere, do you?"

Earl did not, and he was as anxious as his brother. Back and forth they pushed their way, but without success. Then Earl looked at the silver watch he carried. "Ten minutes to twelve!" he ejaculated.

"Let us go on board and stand where Uncle Foster can see us," suggested Randy, in a tone of voice which was far from steady. Supposing their uncle should not turn up, what should they do? To go alone on that trip seemed out of the question.

Luckily they had their tickets, so getting on board

was not difficult. A number of the passengers glanced at them curiously.

"Goin' ter Alaska?" asked one brawny fellow whose face was almost entirely concealed by his tangled beard. "Well, well! Ain't yer most afraid ye'll git done up?"

"We'll try to keep on top," answered Earl. The fellow wished to continue the conversation, but both Earl and Randy were too impatient just then to listen to him, and moved off to another part of the boat.

Five minutes more had passed and an officer was going around shouting: "All ashore that's going! We sail in five minutes!" Those to be left behind began to pass over the gang-plank — it was a hasty handshake and a last good-by on every side. The boys looked at each other doubtfully.

"If he doesn't come —" began Earl, when his quick eye caught sight in the crowd of a hat that he recognized. "Uncle Foster! Uncle Foster Portney! Come on board!" he yelled, at the top of his sturdy lungs.

Mr. Portney, in the jam of people below, heard and looked up. In a moment he had caught sight of his nephews and he shook his hand at them. Soon he was mounting the gang-plank, the last of the passengers to come on board. He was out of breath and gave the boys an odd smile.

"I suppose I gave you a scare," he said. "I didn't

mean to be so late, but those business matters took longer than I intended, and then there was a blockade of street cars and I had to walk it. But we're all right now, I reckon," he added, gazing around. "Good-by to San Francisco! When we see her again may our pockets be lined with gold!" And he took off his soft felt hat and waved it at the crowd on shore.

The boat was now swinging clear of the wharf and thousands of hats and handkerchiefs were waving. "There she goes!" "Hurrah for Alaska!" "If you strike it rich, let us know!" "God be with you!" These and a hundred other cries rang out, and they were kept up until the steamer was far out in the stream and on her way up the bay to the Golden Gate.

The run to the Gate did not take long, and by the middle of the afternoon the steamer was standing out boldly into the Pacific Ocean, on her way almost due north. It had been rather muggy, and now a heavy mist set in, and by evening the boys were glad enough to leave the deck and arrange their stateroom. It contained four berths, two for themselves, one for Mr. Portney, and the last for a stranger who was down on the ship's list as Captain Luke Zoss.

"I wonder who Captain Zoss can be?" said Randy to Earl, when the door of the stateroom was suddenly flung open, and the bushy-bearded man who had spoken to them on deck came in. He stared at them in surprise for a second, then burst into a hearty fit of laughter.

"Wall! wall! So it's you as are goin' ter be my messmates on this yere trip!" he exclaimed. "All right, lads, glad ter have ye." He held out a brawny hand. "My handle is Luke Zoss, but most of the boys know me as Cap'n Luke. May I be so inquisitive as to ask your names?"

"My name is Earl Portney, and this is my brother Randy," answered Earl. The hearty way of the stranger pleased him, and he was sure he should like Zoss.

"Portney, eh? I used ter know a man by thet name — Foster Portney, o' Colorady."

"Why, he's our uncle, and he is with us!" cried Randy, and just then his uncle came in, and he and Captain Zoss shook hands. They had met in Creede, where Zoss had once been a mining superintendent, and knew each other quite well.

"All bound fer the Klondike!" exclaimed the captain. "Hooray! We're sure to strike it, eh, Portney? I know you wouldn't be a-goin' thar unless gold was to be picked up. Goin' over Chilkoot Pass, I take it." Foster Portney nodded. "Then we might as well stick together, eh? It will be better than pairing off with somebody as might be wuss nor a hoss thief, eh? O' course it would!"

Again the captain shook hands. Then he asked the boys where they came from and was pleased to learn they were used to a life in the open air.

"I was a lumberman myself onct — up in Michigan," he said. "But thar wasn't enough excitement, so I gave it up to seek gold and silver. Minin' and prospectin' just suit me — leas'wise so long as the grub holds out. One thing is in our favor — scarcity o' men up in them new gold fields. Now, down in Colorady it's different — all overrun with men, eh, Portney?"

"Yes, we'll have rather an open field," answered Foster Portney. And then followed a long discussion about the new gold fields and what might be expected when Dyea was reached and the terrible climb over the mountains began. The discussion lasted until ten o'clock, and the boys listened with interest and picked up many stray bits of information. Both concluded that the overland trip to the mines would prove every bit as rough and dangerous as they had pictured it.

The distance from San Francisco to Juneau, Alaska, is, in round figures, one thousand miles. The *Golden Hope* was not as large as a regular ocean liner, yet she was a fast boat, and it was expected that she would cover the distance inside of four days. Much, of course, would depend upon the weather encountered, for she was heavily loaded with both passengers and freight. The freight had given even the owners concern, for much of it was piled high on the outer decks.

On the second day out, and some time after Cape Blanco had been sighted through the glass, the sky to the westward began to darken, and the sailors announced an approaching storm. Soon the sun went under a heavy bank of clouds and a stiff breeze sprung up which threw the long, heavy swells of the ocean into millions of white-caps, dancing and skipping on every side as far as eye could reach.

"We are in for it now," was the announcement which went the rounds. Presently it began to rain, and all endeavored to seek the shelter of the cabin, which speedily became crowded to suffocation. The boys, their uncle, and Captain Zoss were in the forward part of the boat, and they saw the course changed, so that the *Golden Hope* stood out straight to meet the blow.

"We are going to have no fun of this," said Foster Portney, with a grave shake of his head. "If I know anything about matters, that storm will be an extra heavy one." And the events of the next hour proved that he was right.

CHAPTER IX.

THE FATE OF A STOWAWAY.

"My gracious! We're going to the bottom sure!"

It was Randy who made the observation. The storm had struck the steamer in all its fury, and the pitching of the vessel made it almost impossible for a person to keep his feet. Randy clutched a handrail fastened near by, and Earl did the same; while Mr. Portney and Captain Zoss braced up against a ceiling post. The only thing that kept many from falling was the fact that there was no vacant floor space. "They were in it like sardines in a tin," as Randy expressed it.

"Some of the outside freight is bound to go," remarked Foster Portney, a minute later. "Ah, as I thought — the captain has ordered it cut away. There goes some poor fellows' outfits! Too bad!"

"I hope our stuff isn't among it!" cried Earl. "But they'll be responsible, won't they?"

"Yes, they'll be responsible, Earl. But we don't want their money — we want our goods, for it may be difficult, if not impossible, to duplicate the things at Juneau. But I imagine **our** goods are in the hold."

"Our clothing and provisions are," said Randy. "I saw them put down just before we started. But the tools may be out there."

"If they —" began Captain Zoss, but broke off short as a mighty crash was heard from the rear deck. The crash was followed by the jingle of broken glass and sharp cries of pain and alarm.

There was every evidence of a panic, but the cooler heads restored order, and then it was found that a miner's outfit had caused all the trouble. It had been loosened from the deck, but before it could be thrown overboard a lurch of the steamer had sent it sailing through the air straight through a cabin window. The miner to whom the outfit belonged had been one of those to be most scared by its unceremonious entrance.

For three hours the storm raged in all its fury, and during that time no one but the officers and crew were allowed on deck. Nearly all the outside freight was thrown away, a loss which amounted to several thousand dollars. At last the wind and the rain gradually abated, and by nightfall the *Golden Hope* was again proceeding on her journey northward.

On the following day they ran by Vancouver Island, and it was calculated that they would reach Juneau by noon of the day following. All were anxious concerning the outfits which had been lost overboard, and the miners and officers tried to make out a list of them.

The work proceeded all day, and it was not until nightfall that it was learned positively that the goods belonging to the Portneys and to Captain Zoss were safe.

The first sight of Juneau was rather disappointing to the boys, who had expected to see a much larger place. Juneau is but a small town, lying on the western coast of a peninsula formed by the Lynn Canal and the wide mouth of the Taku River. Directly opposite is Douglas Island. The town lies on a small patch of flat ground, backed up by several high mountains. It is principally a trading centre. The harbor is a fairly good one, and, on account of the rush to the gold fields, the stores were increasing constantly.

As soon as the steamer reached her landing place a wild rush for shore ensued, and then began a hunt for some vessel which might take the party up to Dyea, where the journey by water would, for the present, come to an end. The water up the Lynn Canal, as it is termed, although it is not at all a canal as we know them, and through Dyea Inlet, is shallow, and, consequently, ocean steamers do not go beyond Juneau.

"I'll hunt up passage on some boat," said Foster Portney to the boys. "You remain here and watch our goods. Those fellows who lost their outfits are angry enough, and some of them would like nothing better than to appropriate ours and let us look to the steamboat company for redress."

While he was gone, **the task** of bringing the goods

from the steamer's hold was started, for no one wanted to be delayed in Juneau any longer than was necessary. Randy and Earl watched the work closely, and as soon as their things appeared they claimed them and had the lot transferred to a spot at the end of the rather rotten and shaky dock.

Presently, as they stood waiting for the reappearance of their uncle and Captain Zoss, who had gone with Mr. Portney, they noticed a commotion on board the *Golden Hope*. A stowaway had been found in the hold of the vessel, and the sailors and stevedores had brought the fellow out more dead than alive.

"Get off of here!" cried the captain of the steamer, in a rage, as he booted the fellow not once, but half a dozen times. "Get out, I say! If we were down in San Francisco I'd have you locked up in a minute. It's a pity I didn't find you out when we were on the trip — I'd a-made you work your passage, and more! Go, before I heave you overboard!"

And with a final kick the stowaway was run off the gang-plank, to fall in a heap on the dock, too weak from the confinement and want of proper food to stand.

"It's Fred Dobson!" ejaculated Randy. "Oh, Earl, look!"

"It is Fred, true enough!" replied Earl, as much surprised as his brother. Forgetful of their outfits for the time being, both ran forward and picked up the son of the squire of Basco. Fred's eyes were closed, his

"WITH A FINAL KICK THE STOWAWAY WAS RUN OFF THE
GANG-PLANK." — *Page 72.*

face was as white as chalk, and they saw at a glance that he had fainted.

"Get some water, Randy," said Earl, as he began to work over the prostrate figure. "I wonder if there is a doctor handy. He looks as if he was half starved to death."

As Randy ran off, a crowd began to collect, a few to sympathize, but the majority to look on merely in curiosity or to make audible comments that it served the boy right, since he had no business to steal a trip.

"Got a crazy notion to go to the gold fields, I reckon," said one bystander. "He ought to be home where his mamma could spank him."

At this there was a coarse laugh, which was quickly hushed when another man, a young fellow of not more than twenty-three, stepped forward, and announced that he was a doctor. He soon succeeded in bringing Fred around.

"He wants something to eat as much as anything," said the newcomer. "There is a restaurant over yonder. Better take him there and get him some soup and stale bread — his stomach isn't strong enough to bear a regular meal."

Randy and Earl thanked the doctor and did as advised, while the crowd gradually melted away to tend to its own affairs. Fred was ravenously hungry, yet he ate with difficulty when the food was set before him.

"I've had nothing to eat for about forty hours," he

said, when he felt strong enough to talk. "I spent that four dollars you two gave me in buying provisions, crackers, cheese, and the like, but on the second day out the rats got at the crackers and cheese and ate nearly the whole of them. Then one of my bottles of water was smashed during that storm, and though it was as close as pepper down there I hadn't a mouthful to drink. I thought I was going to die just before they opened the hold and began to remove the cargo."

"But, Fred, what made you do it?" asked Earl, reproachfully. "It was the height of foolishness."

"I'm bound to go to the gold fields, Earl. You two are going there to make a fortune, and why can't I make a fortune, too?"

"Because you are not fit for life out there, that's why. You suffered a good deal in coming this far, but let me tell you that I expect to suffer a good deal more than that before the Klondike River is reached and we have endured the hardships of an Alaskan winter. Supposing you succeed in getting away up in Alaska and are taken sick, who is going to care for you, and how are you going to get back home? Now I don't want to preach, but my advice is, to go back to Basco at once."

"And that's my advice, too, Fred," broke in Randy. "I know you are as old as I am, but you know you never did such work as Earl and I are used to, and some of the experienced miners even laugh at us. If

Uncle Foster hadn't known that we were used to hard work out in the open, in midwinter at that, he would never have dreamed of asking us to go with him; he told us so."

Randy and Earl both spoke earnestly, and it was not their fault that what they had to say did not take effect. But Fred Dobson was both wild and reckless, and he shook his head.

"I'm bound to go if I have to walk the rest of the way," he said. "I thought I would strike your uncle again when we reached the place, but if you are so dead set against me I'll not say another word, but try to paddle my own canoe, as the saying is. Of course I'm much obliged for what you did for me in San Francisco and here, and some day I'll make it up to you, see if I don't."

"We don't want you to make it up, Fred; only act sensible and steer for home when you next strike out," said Earl. He was about to go on, when the entrance of his uncle and Captain Zoss into the restaurant caused him to stop.

"Humph! so you've turned up again!" were Foster Portney's words. "I heard there had been a stowaway on board of the *Golden Hope*. It was the most foolish move you could make, lad." The prospector turned to his youngest nephew. "Randy, where are our outfits?"

"Oh my!" burst out Randy, leaping to his feet. "Earl, we forgot all about them!"

Earl said nothing, but he reached the door of the restaurant almost as quickly as his brother. There was a crowd in the roadway outside, but they quickly forced a passage through, and ran for the steamer dock. A large number of outfits were spread here, there, and everywhere, but the spot where they had left those belonging to their own party was vacant.

CHAPTER X.

UP THE LYNN CANAL.

RANDY and Earl gazed about them in hopeless bewilderment. The outfits belonging to themselves, their uncle, and to Captain Zoss were gone. Who had taken them, and was there any chance of recovery?

"We should have looked after them," said Earl, bitterly. "It was foolishness to leave the stuff, especially after Uncle Foster had warned us."

"I wonder if any of those miners who lost their outfits from the steamer are guilty," said Randy, as they started on another tour of the Juneau wharf. "I remember one fellow with a red beard and a scar on his nose who looked at the stuff rather closely when we came ashore."

"Let us start to make inquiries, Randy. We must get our outfits back. If we don't, Uncle Foster will never forgive us."

"Yes, and we'll be in a pickle besides," groaned the younger brother. "By the look of things in this settlement mining outfits are rather scarce."

"Yes, I heard one man saying that about everything worth having had been gobbled up several weeks ago and the storekeepers were awaiting new consignments from San Francisco, Portland, and Seattle."

With anxious hearts they walked around the wharf and along a side road, also piled high with miners' goods and steamer freight. Presently a man joined them. It was Captain Zoss.

"Well, whar's our packs?" he questioned, and looked glum when told of what had occurred. "By the boots, lads, we must find 'em — ain't no two ways about that! Why, to go to the mines without tools would be wuss nor a hen sittin' on a nest without eggs. Been all over the dock, yer say?" He paused an instant. "I'll make a round o' the saloons. If the things was stolen, like as not the thieves would want to git 'em out of sight in quick order, eh?"

He was about to leave them, when they were hailed by a man standing near the entrance to a new store that was going up on the opposite side of the way. It was the doctor who had so kindly come to Fred Dobson's assistance.

"What's up?" he called out. "Looking for your traps? They're all right. I had them brought up here for safe keeping when you went off with the sick lad. I knew they wouldn't be secure down on the wharf. There are half a dozen quarrels on down there over lost and mixed-up baggage."

Randy and Earl felt much relieved, and so did the captain. They ran over to the new store, and sure enough, everything was there in a heap, alongside of the packs owned by the doctor. They thanked the medical man for his kindness, and a short talk followed. The doctor's name was Kenneth Barwaithe, and he was an Englishman who had practised for a year in Victoria. He, too, was bound for the new gold fields, either for mining purposes, or to set himself up in business.

"The hundreds of miners going up there will need doctoring," he explained. "And I am all prepared to dose them with medicine, set a broken leg, amputate an arm, or pull an aching tooth."

"Thar'll be work for you," said Captain Zoss, with a laugh. "But the wust disease up thar will be one ye can't touch nohow."

"Indeed! And what is that?" questioned Kenneth Barwaithe, with interest.

"Starvation," was the solemn reply.

In order to relieve their uncle of further anxiety, Randy and Earl returned to where they had left Mr. Portney. They found him in earnest conversation with Fred Dobson. The face of the squire's son was very red and his eyes were downcast.

"I'll write home at once," they heard Fred say, in a low voice. "I'm glad Earl wrote from San Francisco. My folks will at least know I am alive and well — that is, as well as a fellow can be who was half starved to death," he added ruefully.

"And you ought to go home, lad — it's the proper place for you."

"Well, maybe I will — after I have earned enough around here to take me, Mr. Portney."

Foster Portney's hand was in his pocket, and Earl and Randy saw him hand Fred a ten-dollar bill. "Pay me back whenever you feel rich enough to do so," he said, and the squire's son gave him a ready promise to that effect.

Foster Portney and Captain Zoss had been fortunate enough to secure passage up to Dyea, on a little steamboat, which was to leave early the next day. The craft was a freight boat, but carried passengers whenever she could get them. No time was lost in transferring their goods to this craft, Fred Dobson helping them carry their loads. Doctor Barwaithe had also secured passage in the craft, and soon became one of the party. Later on, matters were talked over by him and the others, and it was agreed that the five should stick together until the Klondike region was reached. The forming of little parties of five or more was popular among those who travelled by the overland route into Alaska. By such means there was less danger of a man getting lost in the mountains, and the preparation of meals along the way was easier, for each man of a party took his turn at feeding the rest, so that only one set of packs had to be unstrapped and packed again, instead of the lot. Besides this, the building and sailing of a boat down the lakes and through the rapids by one man was next to impossible.

It was very difficult to obtain accommodations at any of the so-styled hotels in Juneau, so all hands encamped for the night on the deck of the freighter, Fred Dobson managing to smuggle himself in with the regular party. In the morning Fred approached the captain of the boat for a situation, but was turned off in language far from fit to transcribe to these pages.

"Got more on board than we want now, boy, so git ashore in a hurry, for we're on the point of sailing," and with a wistful good-by to Randy, Earl, and the others, the squire's son leaped to the dock. Five minutes later the lines were cast off, and the wheezy, overloaded craft started northward on the Lynn Canal.

The distance from Juneau to Dyea is a hundred and eighteen miles, past Berner's Bay and Katschan River into Chilkoot Inlet and finally up Dyea Inlet. The run for the most part is past gigantic glaciers on one side and mountains covered with snow and ice on the other.

"Gracious, this is a touch of winter and no mistake!" ejaculated Randy, as the steamboat ploughed steadily on her way, and they stood by the rail taking in the desolate sight. "See how those little icebergs sparkle in the sunshine."

"Far off to the west of this canal is the great Muir

Glacier," said Foster Portney. "It is the largest glacier in the world. That island which we just passed is Douglas, and there is situated the great Treadwell Mine, one of the richest gold mines heretofore discovered in Alaska."

"Have we got to climb mountains like that?" questioned Earl, as he pointed to the snow-capped summits to the eastward.

"Have we got to climb 'em?" burst in Captain Zoss. "Why, them ain't an ant hill to the ones we're to crawl over, lad. Just wait till we get up into Dyea Inlet, and you'll catch sight o' mountains as will give you the yellow shakes, as the boys call it. Now I don't want to discourage ye," he went on, as he saw Earl take a deep breath. "I want to prepare ye for the wust, that's all. That pass — the Chilkoot — is the wust part o' the whole trip, being about three-quarters of a mile high and betwixt mountains twice that size."

"Well, we can climb three-quarters of a mile, I guess, if the grade isn't too steep," said Randy.

The captain turned away and smiled to himself. He was more than doubtful if the boys would ever get safely over to Lake Linderman, the first of the lakes on the other side of the mountain range.

It was well that they had dressed themselves warmly; for, on account of the sun shining on the glaciers the air was filled with a mist which chilled them to the bone. The channel was filled with loose pieces of ice, and ever and anon the steamer would strike a miniature iceberg with a crash which was clearly heard by all on board.

After a few hours of gazing at the monotonous presentation of glaciers and snow-covered hills and mountains, the boys turned their attention to those on board. It was a motley collection of people. Most of the men were Americans, but there was also a fair sprinkling of Canadians, Germans, and half a dozen Indians. The latter were of the Chilkoot tribe, and interested Randy more than anything else. They were a round-faced, stalwart set of fellows, and several of them had bands of black painted across the upper parts of their faces.

"They paint the black around their eyes as a preventive of snow-blindness," explained Foster Portney. "As soon as either of you find your eyes hurting from the glare you had better put on a pair of the smoked goggles."

Dinner on the steamer was served under the rather scanty shelter on the upper deck. But fifteen could be accommodated at once, and as there were over sixty people on board, it took some time to satisfy them all. The fare was principally beef stew, bread, coffee, and rice pudding, but the cold air gave every one a good appetite, and the boys did full justice to all that was offered them.

At turning-in time there was more than one little row, for sleeping accommodations were limited. Berths were at a premium, and had been secured by the more fortunate ones when the steamer had landed at Juneau. Foster Portney gathered his party around him in the shelter of the wheelhouse, on deck, and here they slept huddled together like sheep in a cattle car.

"Not like stopping at the Palace Hotel in San Francisco, is it?" said his uncle to Randy. "But never mind; as soon as we leave Dyea we'll have all the room we want, and more."

"Sleeping like this keeps a fellow warm," said Randy, who felt somehow as if he was out for a lark. But by and by, when somebody passed over him in the dark and slipped on his chest, he did not think it quite so much fun.

However, the night passed quickly enough, and at daybreak all were stirring, for they had reached Dyea Inlet, and a landing was expected before noon. A stiff breeze was blowing, and the Inlet, a long, narrow arm of Chilkoot Inlet and the canal, was filled with angry waves blowing from off shore. Presently the first sight of Dyea was gained, and half an hour later an anchor was dropped, and the voyage so far as the steamer was concerned was over.

CHAPTER XI.

THE START FROM DYEA.

RANDY and Earl found Dyea but a small settlement. There was one store which had been established for some time, and half a dozen others which had sprung up to accommodate the miners and adventurers who were pouring into the place. The total white population did not number a hundred, but there were a very large number of Indians, — men, women, and children, — all anxious to obtain employment as pack-carriers over the mountains.

The steamer had anchored some distance from the beach, and it was no light work to get the packs ashore in the heavy sea that was running. Four small boats were employed for the purpose, and more than one bundle was lost overboard in making the transfer to land.

"There goes one of my packs!" suddenly sang out Dr. Barwaithe, as a small boat loaded high above the gunwales capsized just as the shore was struck. A wild scramble by the miners was made to recover their goods. The doctor would have gone into the icy water also, but he could not swim.

Several Indians who were watching the scene, rushed up to the medical man. "Get heem fo' one dolla!" said the largest of the redmen, and the doctor made the bargain on the spot. At once the Indian and his helper leaped into the surf and swam toward the pack, which contained the doctor's clothing and bedding, and was becoming rapidly water soaked. They reached the pack as it was about to sink, and after ten minutes of hard work brought it out on the pebbly shore.

By the middle of the afternoon all hands found themselves encamped along the half-dried-up stream back of the settlement. Here there were nearly a hundred tents of miners and prospectors who were not quite ready to attempt the trip over Chilkoot Pass.

The Indian who had rescued the doctor's pack stuck to the medical man for the job of transferring his goods over to Lake Linderman, stating he and his companions would do the work for fifteen cents a pound.

"What do you think of that rate?" asked Dr. Barwaithe of Foster Portney, while Randy and Earl looked on with interest.

"I don't know but that it's fair enough," was the reply.

"But wouldn't it be better to take horses from here and use Indians only over the pass? You know we have about thirteen miles to travel before the pass is reached."

"We had better take the Indians from here," put in Captain Zoss. "Thar's no tellin' if we can git 'em further on, eh?"

"Yes, and we might as well get used to walking it from here, too," added Mr. Portney. "It will do Randy and Earl some good, not but that I imagine they can tramp as well as any of us."

"We've tramped for many a mile through the Maine woods, when we were out hunting," said Randy. "By the way," he went on, "I haven't seen any game yet, outside of a few birds."

The big Indian, who rejoiced in the name of Salmon Head, was waiting for an answer, his squaw and two boys standing close by. The squaw was a tall, thin woman of forty, whose face was painted a greasy black down to the tip of her nose, the balance of her countenance being left its natural color, yellowish red. The boys were sturdy lads of perhaps ten and twelve, as used to carrying heavy burdens as their parents.

The bargain was struck with Salmon Head to have the goods of the entire party packed over from that spot to the shore of Lake Linderman for fifteen cents a pound, the work to be accomplished within the next four days, weather permitting. The boys had expected to carry some of the goods, but at this Foster Portney shook his head.

"You couldn't carry over forty or fifty pounds and maybe not that over the Pass," he said, "and I would rather pay the price and have you reserve your strength. You can each carry a knapsack filled with food, in case you wander from the trail, although don't let this happen if you can possibly avoid it. The best rule, in going over any pass, is to keep at least two other members of the party in sight constantly."

In spite of the close proximity of the snow-capped mountains, the night was a comparatively warm one, and no inconvenience was experienced by the party in their tents. They had two, one belonging to Mr. Portney and the boys, the other being one Captain Zoss and Dr. Barwaithe had purchased at Juneau for mutual comfort. The tents were put up end to end, and being both water and wind tight were almost as good to sleep in as a cabin.

The outfits had been carefully parcelled out to the Indians, Salmon Head carrying a load of over a hundred and twenty-five pounds, his squaw carrying a hundred pounds, and the sons loads of about half that weight. Relatives of these Indians carried the remainder of the loads; for these Chilkoot people, like other redmen, believed in keeping all they could in the family.

Usually the journey to Lake Linderman was made in two stages, the first from Dyea to the entrance to Chilkoot Pass, and the second over the Pass itself and down to the lake, which may fairly be called the southern headwaters of the Yukon River. This course was to be pursued by the present party, and bright and early on the following morning they started out on what was destined to be the most perilous trip of their lives. Captain Zoss went ahead with the Indians, while the boys and their uncle and the doctor kept in a bunch behind.

At the start, the trip was along the bottom of a deep cañon, on either side of which arose mountains and cliffs for the most part covered with snow and ice. Down in this cañon flowed what is called the Dyea River, a mere mountain torrent, dashing over rocks and crags and here and there broadening out into a shallow flow over sand and pebbles. Walking was rough, for at times they had to leap from one great rock to another or else let themselves down, to wade through water and sand up to their knees. The wind had calmed down, yet once in a while it sent upon them a flurry of fine snow from the distant mountain tops.

"We are not getting ahead very fast!" puffed Randy, as he and the others came to a halt on a flat rock to rest. "We've been walking for three hours, and I doubt if we have covered more than five miles."

"I heard at Dyea that the thirteen miles to the entrance to the Pass is considered a good day's journey," said Earl. "I'm rather glad I'm not carrying that load Salmon Head has strapped to his back."

"It would take me a week to get that load up," said

Randy. "I can't understand how those boys get along."

"It's a matter of training," said Foster Portney. "I dare say either of you can cut down a tree in half the time that those Chilkoots can do it."

On they went again, the trail now growing steeper and more barren. A few stunted firs lined the cañon, and here and there could be seen a half-dead vine twisted about the fir branches, and that was all, so far as vegetation went. And this was coming summer time!

"It must be dreariness itself in winter," remarked Earl, to his uncle, as they trudged along side by side. "I never saw anything so desolate, not even in the wildest parts of Maine."

"It is this desolate look which has kept men out of Alaska, Earl. Many have known of there being gold there, but they preferred to remain down in the States, where living, at least, was more certain and congenial. You'll find, my lad, that you will need all your nerve and backbone to withstand what is before you. Perhaps I did wrong in urging you to join me."

"No, you didn't — I'm glad I came, and so is Randy, and we'll get through," answered Earl, hastily. "Oh, look!" he pointed to where a flock of birds were circling far overhead. "Shall I give them a shot?"

"No! no!" cried Foster Portney, hastily. "I forgot to tell you. I arranged with the Indians that no shot should be fired on the trip excepting some one was in trouble and needed assistance. I'll inform the others." And he halted for the others to come up.

Captain Zoss provided the dinner at about one o'clock, all hands taking it easy on some clear rocks in the sunshine. As may be supposed, the fare was a plain one, yet to Randy and Earl nothing had ever tasted better, for climbing and the bracing mountain air gave them enormous appetites. They could have eaten more than was provided but understood that from henceforth until further supplies were assured, rations would be dealt out with a sparing hand.

As soon as the dinner dishes had been cleaned and repacked the journey to Sheep Camp, as the stopping-place was called, was renewed. The trail was now steeper than ever, and more than once the stream of water had to be crossed. Every one was suffering from wet feet, but as all had on several pairs of heavy socks, this did no further damage than to render them cold in their nether limbs. As the trail grew rougher the Indians, who knew every footstep, forged ahead, and the others were allowed to shift for themselves.

It was about the middle of the afternoon that Randy and his uncle were walking one behind the other, with Captain Zoss and Dr. Barwaithe just in the rear. The captain had been relating one of his experiences in mountain climbing in Colorado, to which all had listened with interest. The story was finished, and they were congratulating themselves that the end of the day's tramp was close at hand, when Randy suddenly looked around in alarm.

"Where is Earl?" he asked

"Earl!" exclaimed Mr. Portney. "Why, he is ahead, isn't he?"

"No, he dropped behind, to fix his boot," was the quick reply. "Earl! Earl!"

The cry was repeated, and the others also took it up. Then they waited for an answer, but none came. Earl had disappeared. They waited for five minutes for him to make his reappearance, but he did not come; and then they started on a search for him.

CHAPTER XII.

EARL HAS AN ADVENTURE.

As Randy had explained, Earl had stopped on the trail to fix his boot. In crossing the mountain stream he had shipped a lot of water, and he sat down on a rock and held up his foot, to allow the water to run out on the ground.

Unfortunately for the youth he had rested on a rock which was by no means secure on the bank of the stream, and now, as he leaned to one side, the rock slipped from its resting-place, and down went poor Earl into the water head first. As luck would have it, he struck in some loose sand, otherwise he would have been seriously injured. Even as it was he was stunned for the moment, and before he could turn he had gulped down a great deal of water. He was nearly blinded by some fine sand getting into his eyes and began to flounder around as though in the midst of an ocean instead of a watercourse less than fifty feet wide and five feet deep.

It took several minutes for him to save himself by reaching a large rock in the centre of the stream.

Collecting his scattered senses, he cleared his eyes as best he could and took a view of his situation.

The rock was six feet in diameter and two feet above the top of the water. On either side flowed the stream at a rate which he knew would be quite sufficient to take him off his feet should he attempt to ford to shore. What was to be done in this emergency he did not at first know. The others had gone on ahead, and although he called to them, no one heard his cry.

Had he had his gun he would have fired it, had the weapon been in condition. But less than quarter of an hour before he had passed the fowling-piece over to Captain Zoss, the captain having asked to inspect it. He must help himself, or go without assistance.

Standing on the rock, he saw that escape to either side was out of the question, and escape up the stream was also cut off. Below, however, were a series of rocks running off to shore, and after some hesitation he dropped into the stream and allowed himself to be carried down to these rocks.

Five minutes of struggling in the current found him safe on the opposite shore to that upon which the lower portion of the trail to Chilkoot Pass lay. The question now was, how to get back to the other side of the river.

"I'll walk along on this side until I get a chance to cross over," he said, half aloud, and then the loneliness of his situation dawned upon him. He struck out without delay, determined to catch up with the others of the party as quickly as possible.

For the first quarter of a mile Earl did very well, but soon he noted to his dismay that the stream was widening, and that, consequently, he was getting further and further away from the other side. He had been making his way along a cliff lined with short firs. Now the cliff came to an abrupt end, and beyond he beheld nothing but a mass of jagged rocks and a jungle of brush, to pass through which would be next to impossible.

"Stumped now!" he muttered to himself, and his face fell as he surveyed his situation. The stream at this point was all of one hundred and fifty feet wide, and the trail opposite was not close to the water's edge, but wound in behind the rocks and fir trees.

"I've got to get over to that trail, that's certain!" he went on, after a disagreeable pause. "Here goes to try the water again," and with extreme care he began the descent of the cliff, which was some twenty feet high. The bottom was reached in safety, and he found himself standing in water and sand half up to his knees.

Because of the widening of the stream at this point the current was not so strong, and he began to wade in deeper and deeper, until one-quarter of the width had been passed and he found himself up to his waist. He shivered with the cold and felt like going back, but a few steps more brought him to a sand-bar, where the water scarcely touched his knees. Overjoyed at this, he attempted to follow up the bar, soon reaching and passing the middle of the river. He was wading on more confidently than ever, when of a sudden the bar came to an end, and down he plunged into a pool over his head.

The one thing to do now was to swim, and Earl struck out boldly for the shore, still thirty feet away. The weight of his heavy clothing was against him, and the current carried him on and on down the stream and toward a mass of jagged rocks fearful to behold. Had he been of a less rugged temperament the cold water might have given him both a chill and a cramp.

Five minutes of fearful anxiety passed, and Earl was almost exhausted, when, putting his foot down, he struck bottom at a depth of four feet. This encouraged him, and he renewed his effort to reach the bank beyond. Yet another pool had to be crossed, and when finally he did pull himself out of the stream and safe up on a sloping rock he was too exhausted to do aught but lie down on his side and pant for breath.

It was here that Randy and his uncle found him, just as he was making an effort to gain his feet and continue his search for them. They were overjoyed to learn that he had not suffered serious injury. They called to Captain Zoss and Dr. Barwaithe, who were close by, and soon all were together again.

Captain Zoss had an extra shirt in his pack, and this

Earl borrowed, along with a dry coat belonging to his uncle. Both articles of wearing apparel were too large for him, but he gladly exchanged them, for the time being, for his wet ones; and then the delayed journey toward Sheep Camp was continued.

When the resting-place for the night was gained, it was found that all of the Indians had come in over an hour before and had sought out a comfortable camp for them under a large overhanging rock. A number of others had also arrived, and over a dozen tents had been pitched in addition to those already there. According to lot, it was Randy's turn to get a meal ready, and he set to work without delay, starting a roaring fire of pine branches and logs, that Earl might warm and dry himself. Dr. Barwaithe had brought with him a newly patented sheet-iron camp stove, and on this a pot of water was soon boiling, to be used in making coffee, while Randy also offered them fried potatoes and a deliciously cooked fish one of the Indians brought in.

Outside of the doctor, who was not used to walking over such rough ground, no one felt any ill effects of the day's journey, although all were glad to turn in at the earliest possible moment. The doctor had worn a slight blister on his heel, and, in order to prevent this giving him serious concern later, he put some salve on it and bound it up before retiring.

Ere they crawled into the tent, both boys took a look

at the great, white mountains, which loomed up before them. Here was the entrance to Chilkoot Pass, and there, almost lost among the clouds, was the dreaded summit, with mountains still higher on either side of it. Randy drew closer to Earl as he surveyed the awe-inspiring scene.

"Earl, we've got an everlasting hard climb before us," he whispered. "Do you think we'll make it?"

"We must make it, Randy," was the low and earnest reply. "It won't do to show the white feather now. Uncle would never forgive us."

"Some parts of it look like crawling up the side of a house," and Randy shuddered. "If a fellow should fall, he'd break his neck sure."

"I guess you're right, Randy; although it may not be so bad when one is right on top of it. There is a sort of a trail, you know, although it's not much. I heard Salmon Head tell Uncle he hoped it would be cold to-morrow night, and that we should start for the Pass about four or five o'clock in the afternoon. I wonder what he meant by that."

"I heard Captain Zoss speaking of it. They start toward evening so as to pass the deepest snows on the summit about midnight when a crust forms to walk on, for at this season of the year the deep snows are too soft to be trusted when the sun is shining."

"And what happens to a fellow, I wonder, if he breaks through the snow?"

"I don't know, I'm sure — I guess he goes to kingdom come," and Randy shuddered again. "We'll know all about it by this time to-morrow night." And then both boys retired, to dream of perilous climbs over the snow-clad mountains and fearful falls into gigantic crevasses, until both awoke in a fright and covered with cold perspiration.

It was not until late that anybody was stirring the next day. It was Earl's turn to get breakfast, and he told them if they would wait he would treat them to freshly baked beans and hot bread; and all waited. While Earl was at work, with Randy helping him, two of the Indian boys came up, and their efforts at making themselves understood were laughable. Finally Randy made out that they wanted an old silk neckerchief he possessed, and he gave it to Tomablink, the older youth, who was as proud of the article as if it had been worth a small fortune.

Under the advice of Foster Portney, all took it easy in camp that day, in order to reserve their strength for the struggle to come. Even the Indians seemed to grow a bit uneasy concerning what was before them; for, although they had climbed over the Pass a number of times, they well knew what a rough and highly dangerous proceeding each new trip was likely to be. On this terrible Pass more than one Indian and white man had been lost, never to be heard of again.

At last, at exactly four o'clock in the afternoon,

Salmon Head announced his readiness to start. As chief of the Indian party, he had looked to it that each carrier's pack was properly adjusted, and now he gave several directions to the whites to the effect that they should keep together as much as possible and always in sight of his own people.

"Don't think there be an easy this way or that," he said in broken English. "Indian know best way in the end — you follow him day and night, or you lost. Stick foot deep down when climb, and no let go with hands."

His manner was so earnest, all promised to remember his words. Then the crowd of whites and Indians was gathered together, the tents were struck and packed; and the terrifying journey over the dreadful Chilkoot Pass was begun.

CHAPTER XIII.

AT THE SUMMIT OF CHILKOOT PASS.

At Sheep Camp, which lay in something of a hollow, there had been a goodly collection of trees and brush, but now, as the little party started on the journey to the summit of Chilkoot Pass, all this was left behind, and nothing confronted them but immense beds or glaciers of snow, which crunched under their feet and gave forth a hollow sound. At certain points they could plainly hear the rushing of water far beneath.

"Gracious, if a fellow went through this crust of snow what would happen to him?" said Randy, as he trudged on, with his uncle just ahead of him and Earl behind.

"Let us hope that no such fate overtakes any of the party," replied Mr. Portney, gravely. "It is not likely that one can break through here," he added, "for the snow in the trail is pretty well packed down."

The blinding glare of the sun had caused all to put on their smoked glasses, or goggles, but now, as the great orb of day was lost to sight behind the mountain tops, these protectors for the eyes were removed, that they might see their way clearer. The Alaskan twilight was creeping on them, causing all their surroundings to turn to a pale blue color. The mists of the mountains were also rising, and on every hand were weird, ghostlike shadows which enhanced this scene of wild desolation.

On and on went the white members of the party, doing their best to keep the sturdy Indian pack-carriers well in sight. But the red people, with their hideously painted faces, knew every foot of the way, and made rapid progress, and it was all the others could do at times to keep up.

By ten o'clock it began to grow colder, and even the boys could feel the crust of snow on which they were trudging becoming firmer beneath their feet. It was far from dark, a pale glimmer of light hanging on every mountain top. But now the trail became suddenly steeper, and they found themselves going straight up the side of a hill several hundred feet high.

"Plant your feet firmly at every step," were Foster Portney's words of caution. "And remember, looking back will do you no good."

This last warning was for Randy's benefit, for the lad had just looked back and shivered over the awful descent below him. A fall would mean a long roll, and a broken neck over a cliff below.

Captain Zoss had gone on ahead with the Indians and just before midnight he came back with a warning to watch out for several splits, or crevasses, in the glaciers they were now traversing.

"Salmon Head says he heard a report of several new ones just before starting, and these are as yet unmarked," he said.

"We'll be as careful as we can," said Dr. Barwaithe. "We can do no more."

They now passed over a broad plain of snow where the mists hung more thickly than ever. They had almost reached the centre of the plain when a loud cry from the Indians ahead caused them to halt.

"What can be the meaning of that?" questioned Earl. "Can they be in trouble?"

Presently, from among the mists appeared the form of one of the Indian carriers, without his bundle. He soon explained in broken English that he had been sent back by Salmon Head to warn them of a split in the ice field just ahead. One of the Indian women had slipped in, and it was by mere good fortune that some of the men had rescued her.

This Indian remained with them until the crack was reached, where he resumed his pack and went on. The opening was an irregular one, from four to eight feet wide and of unfathomable depth. Fortunately the sides were well defined and firm, so they had small trouble in leaping across.

"It was good of them to send a man back," said the doctor, as he paused to peer down into the crevasse. "Had we not been warned we might have slipped into that without knowing it."

The trail now wound in and out among a number of small hills, and once again the party ahead was lost to sight. With the increasing cold came a stiff wind through the passes, bringing down upon their heads a veritable storm of snow, swept from the mountain tops above.

"I can readily understand how impossible it would be to make one's way through this Pass during the winter," said Dr. Barwaithe. "A regular fall of snow would mean a blizzard down here and a snowing in from which there would be no escape until spring arrived."

"And think of the cold!" said Earl. "Phew! the thermometer must go to about forty below zero!"

"It does go as low as that at times," replied his uncle. "No; travelling through this Pass during the long Alaskan winter is entirely out of the question. The man to undertake it would be a madman."

They had come to the end of the comparatively level portion of the trail, and now climbing so dangerous was at hand that little more was said. From one steep icy elevation they would crawl to the next, until several hundred feet up. Then came a turn around a cliff where the passageway was scarcely two feet wide, with a wall on one side and what appeared misty, bottomless space on the other. Here the Indians had fastened a hand-rope which each was glad enough to clutch as he wormed his way along to safer ground.

"Well, I don't want any more of that!" said Earl, with a long sigh of relief. "A slip there, and it would be good-by, sure!"

"Yes, and I guess they would never even get your body," added Randy.

There was no time left to halt, for the Indians were pressing on, their endurance, and especially the endurance of the women and the boys, proving a constant wonder to Randy and Earl, the latter declaring that they must be tougher than pine knots to stand it.

"One more big climb, boys, and we'll be at the summit!" was the welcome announcement made by Captain Zoss; but when Earl and Randy looked at the climb he mentioned their hearts fairly sank within them and they wondered how in the world they were going to make it without its costing them their lives.

An almost sheer wall of ice and snow confronted them, rising in an irregular form to a height of four hundred feet. This cliff, if such it might be called, was more light at its top than at the base, and consequently it appeared to stand out towards them as they gazed up at it. Along the face the Indian pack-carriers were crawling, like flies on a lumpy whitewashed wall.

"We can't do — " began Randy, when he felt his arm pinched by Earl.

"We must do it, Randy," came back in a whisper. "The Indians are doing it, and so can we — if we'll put our grit into it."

"Now take it slow and be sure of one foot before you move the next," said Foster Portney, warning them again. "Dig as deeply into the ice and snow as you can. And above all things, Randy and Earl, *don't look back!*" And the uncle shook his fist to emphasize his words.

A breathing spell was taken, and then they started slowly for the base of the cliff, where Captain Zoss got down on his knees to make sure that they were on the right trail, if trail it could be called. He soon announced that one party had gone up at one place and the others at a spot about thirty feet to the left.

"I'll try my luck here," he said, and the doctor agreed to follow him. There was no telling which trail was the better, and the Portneys took the other, Mr. Portney going first, with Randy next and Earl last. The uncle wished to make sure of the footing before he allowed the boys to come after him.

The first hundred feet up were not as difficult as Randy and Earl had imagined, but now every step had to be calculated, and when half way up Foster Portney came to a halt.

"Here's a very steep place," he announced, without,

however, looking back. "Randy, when you reach it, catch hold of the spur of ice with your left hand and put your foot just beneath it. Tell Earl to do the same."

"I will," answered Randy, but when the spot mentioned was reached poor Randy's heart leaped into his throat. The sheer wall before him was nearly as high as a house, and there was nothing to cling to but little lumps of ice which stuck out here and there. The lumps might crack off, and then — he did not dare to think further than that. He was strangely tempted to look below him, but his uncle's words of warning rang in his ears — "*Don't look back!*" and he did not.

One step was taken, and then another, and Randy felt as if he was suspended in the air, with nothing above or beneath him. A brief vision of himself lying mangled far below flashed across his mind, and he wished himself safe back in the woods of Maine again. What was all the gold in Alaska worth alongside of such an agonizing risk of life as this?

But he must go on; he could not remain where he was forever. The next step was even more difficult, and he held his breath as he took it. He had been climbing up the cliff for less than quarter of an hour, yet he felt a year older than when he had begun. Would the climb never come to an end?

"Take it easy, boys; we are almost there," came the encouraging voice of Foster Portney, although the uncle was almost as fearful as his nephews. "A little to the right now, and beware of those snow lumps; they are not firm enough to hold to. I can see the top just above my head. Ah, here I am. Now, Randy, another step and give me your hand. Now, Earl, take the same step Randy took. There you are. Thank God we are safe so far!"

The two boys echoed their uncle's sentiment, with a deep feeling in their hearts which they never forgot. The summit of Chilkoot Pass had been reached at last.

CHAPTER XIV.

BOAT-BUILDING AT LAKE LINDERMAN.

THE Portneys, having reached the highest point of Chilkoot Pass, were presently joined by Captain Zoss and Dr. Barwaithe, who had gone through a similar experience to that just described. The doctor had once come very close to losing his footing, and he declared that he would not make the climb again for a million dollars.

They stopped for a few minutes to view the scene from the edge of the cliff. On either side were the still taller mountains, while below them stretched that portion of the Pass just travelled, like a valley of glittering ice, thick with mist and wind-swept snow. An intense silence reigned, broken occasionally by the booming and crunching of some immense glacier in the distance.

"A grand scene, but one not particularly suited to my feelings," said the doctor. "Let us go on."

"Yes; the sooner we git out o' this yere Pass, the better I will be pleased," added the captain. "I've had enough climbin' ter last me two lifetimes, eh?"

and he gave a grunt and strode off, and the others followed.

"That is, I believe, the most perilous part of the trip to the gold fields," remarked Foster Portney. "Of course we have still a good bit of rough country to traverse and rapids in the rivers to shoot, but nothing quite so bad as that."

The ice fields from the summit sloped gradually downward to a basin some distance below, called Crater Lake. This little lake was frozen solid from top to bottom and covered with snow. It was hemmed in on three sides by tall mountains, while on the fourth there was a cañon-like opening, where an ice-bound stream led the way over rocks and tiny cliffs to Lake Linderman, at the end of the Pass. Just before reaching the latter lake, they passed several large posts set up close to the trail, which was now once more clearly defined.

"Those are surveyors' posts," said Foster Portney, in reply to a question from Earl. "We have just passed from United States into British territory."

"This, then, is the Northwest Territory," said Earl.

"Yes, my boy; and the entire Klondike region, from Ogilvie to Belle Isle, is in that territory."

As they descended to the lower level of the Pass, the solid ice gave way to rotten ice and slush, in which they frequently sank to their ankles. Here the stream broadened out into several ponds, and finally ended in a wide, marshy expanse, forming the upper end of Lake Linderman. Along the edge of this marsh they picked their way, first, however, stopping for dinner, for the night had passed and the forenoon had been consumed in the journey from Crater Lake. The Indians kept pressing on, and they followed.

It was dark again when they came up at last with their pack-carriers encamped under some timber, which stood on a little bluff not over two hundred feet from the lake. Salmon Head's party had started a rousing fire, and this was a welcome sight, for it made all feel more at home. No time was lost in getting out the cooking utensils and the doctor's stove; and while they were preparing other things, the Indians brought several fish from the lake to be baked.

"I guess we'll get our fill of fish before long," remarked Earl.

"Don't you want any now?" smiled his uncle.

"Want any, Uncle Foster? Indeed I do! Why, I'm so hungry I could almost eat horse meat!" was Earl's earnest reply; and he bustled around with the cups and plates, that they might not be delayed as soon as the coffee, biscuits, and fish were done.

The Indians remained near by all night, and early in the morning a general reckoning-up took place, and the pack-carriers were paid off in gold and silver, not caring to take the paper money which was offered. All had done very well, and Foster Portney, Captain Zoss, and Dr. Barwaithe did not dispute the amounts asked, although they were a trifle high. As soon as they were paid off, the Indians packed up their own articles, but a handful in number, and hurried away in the direction whence they had come.

"Good gracious! are they going right back to Dyea?" exclaimed Randy, in amazement.

"Yes, my lad," was Captain Zoss's answer. "Salmon Head calculates to pilot another lot o' miners over as soon as possible. It's his hayin' time, ye see, an' he intends ter make the most o' it."

At this Earl laughed. "I guess he's not going to let his legs get stiff," he cried. "I'm as stiff as an old mule this morning. What's to do to-day?"

"We'll locate some timber for boat-building," said his uncle, "and get our traps into shape, and then rest. There is no use in killing ourselves all at once. We've got a matter of five hundred miles to journey yet."

"If we go up into the timber, I suppose we can try our hand at shooting something if anything turns up," said Randy.

"Certainly; shoot all the game you can, boys. We'll want it to help eke out our stores."

There were numerous odds and ends to do about

the camp, and it was not until after dinner that they started into the timber to select some wood which might be used in boat-building. It was now that the boys' knowledge of timber stood them in good stead; and it took but a short while to pick out a tree which was close-grained and comparatively free from knots. They had brought their axes with them, and had the tree down in short order. Then they lopped off the branches and cut off the top, and left it in the sun to dry out as much as possible before attacking it with their boat-building tools.

This accomplished, Earl and Randy set off, the former with the shot-gun and the other with his pistol, to stir up whatever might be around in the way of game. They followed the edge of the cliff to where it sloped down to the lake shore.

Presently Earl thought he saw something in the brush along the water front, and, taking up a half-decayed stick, he threw it at the spot. At once there was a squawk, and half a dozen wild geese arose in the air. Bang! went the shot-gun, and crack! went Randy's pistol, and three of the geese were seen to throw back their heads and sink.

"We hit 'em!" cried Randy, and ran down, followed by his brother. Two of the fowls were dead, and the other was speedily put out of its misery by Earl with a blow from the gun-stock. They had been cautioned not to waste their ammunition, so had not ventured a second round at the balance of the flock.

"These ought to make good eating," observed Randy, as he picked up the game. "That is, if they don't taste too fishy. Here is my bullet hole, right through the neck. You killed the other two."

With the dead geese over their shoulders, they continued their hunt for game, and presently stirred up a number of wild birds, at which Earl blazed away, bringing down five. The birds were small and hardly worth the trouble of cleaning and cooking, yet they took them along.

"Geese, eh?" exclaimed Captain Zoss, as they entered camp. "Wall, that's not so bad! We kin have a goose pot-pie o' one, and stuff the other with bread an' beans, eh?" All hands agreed this would be an excellent plan, and the boys set about cleaning the game without delay, the captain assisting them at the work.

Toward night they espied a band of Indians coming down the trail with their packs and followed by half a dozen miners, a hardy but not an evil-looking crowd. The miners had left Dyea twenty-four hours later than themselves and had brought with them the material for a flat-bottomed scow, fifteen feet long and four feet wide. The Indians had carried this material over the Pass, but how it had been accomplished was a mystery to the boys and the others.

"Hang me, if I don't reckon they have a secret way o' their own," was Captain Zoss's comment. "They couldn't cart them boards up that steep cliff, nohow!" And Randy and Earl were half inclined to believe the captain's suspicions to be true.

The miners, who went by the name of the Idaho crowd, because they came from that State, encamped next to the doctor's crowd, as they were speedily termed, on account of having a medical man with them, and all became well acquainted before night. The Idaho crowd had just heard of an extra large find being made on Gold Bottom Creek, which flowed into the Klondike River, and they were anxious to get up there without delay, and consequently spent half the night in putting their boat together for an early start on the following morning.

"You're the fust boys I've heerd tell on bound for the gold diggin's," said one of the men to Randy and Earl. "I'm afeard ye'll find it kinder tough luck, for as far ez I kin understand it is tough even on a man. Whar are ye from? Californy?"

"No, from the backwoods of Maine," answered Earl. "And we are used to roughing it."

"Gee shoo! Didn't know the news had struck out so all-fired far ez thet. Wall, if you're from the backwoods, 'tain't likely you'll suffer ez much ez some of the tenderfoots wot's older. Wish ye the best o' luck." And the man turned away to his boat-building again.

Eight o'clock of the following morning found the Idaho crowd on its way down Lake Linderman. In the meantime the boys, Foster Portney, and Captain Zoss had started into the timber with their tools, leaving Dr. Barwaithe to watch camp and bake several days' supply of bread and biscuits, and also to parboil some beans for baking.

The tree selected for cutting up had been allowed to fall over a large flat rock, and now the first work was to prop up the lower end. This done, both ends were sawed off even and a good portion of the bark was scaled off. Then Earl and Randy sharpened up several wedges and tried their hands at splitting up the trunk into a suitable size for whipsawing.

This was no light work, and had they not had a knowledge of woodcraft it would have been next to impossible to do what the lads, aided by their uncle and the captain, accomplished. By nightfall the tree was split and sawed up into more than a dozen slabs, of varying thickness, and these were laid out for working up in the morning.

When the party returned to the edge of the lake they found that three other crowds had come in over the Pass, and there was quite a settlement of tents alongshore. In one of the parties there was a young woman, the wife of a prospector, who had stood the arduous climb nearly as well as any one.

"Hullo, Portney!" suddenly cried a voice to Earl,

as he was walking around among the tents. "I didn't know you had got this far."

Earl turned swiftly, and was nearly dumfounded to find himself confronted by Tom Roland, while Jasper Guardley stood but a few feet away.

CHAPTER XV.

ON TO LAKE BENNETT.

THE face of Tom Roland wore a smile, but in his eyes was an anxious look which Earl did not fail to notice as he surveyed the two acquaintances from Basco. The young prospector was much taken aback by this sudden appearance, for he had not dreamed of meeting Roland and Guardley in this out-of-the-way spot.

"Ain't you glad to see a feller from Maine?" went on Roland, as Earl did not speak; and he held out his hand, which the youth took rather coldly. Guardley had come up to shake hands too, but now he did not risk making the offer.

"Are you two bound for the Klondike?" at length asked Earl.

"Of course," was Roland's sharp reply. "What else would we be doing up here?"

"What started you — the fact that we were going?"

"Well, I allow as that had a little to do with it, Earl; but Guardley got a letter from a friend of his who is up there now — a man named Stephens. He said Guardley ought to come up at once, and as he didn't want to go alone, I came along. How are you making out?"

"We are doing very well."

"You and your brother came on with your uncle, didn't you?"

"Yes."

"Any others in the party?"

"Yes; two men."

Tom Roland's eyes dropped for a moment. "Me and Guardley have been havin' rather a hard road of it, all alone," he went on. "We've been thinking of joining forces with somebody."

"Well, our crowd is complete," answered Earl, quickly.

"Then you won't consider taking in two more, providing, of course, we do our share of work and pay our share of the expenses."

"I don't think so, Roland."

"Who is at the head of your party?"

"Nobody in particular; we all work together."

"Maybe you had better speak to the boy's uncle," put in Guardley. "Come on."

He stalked off, and after some slight hesitation Tom Roland followed, with Earl at his side. Foster Portney was found mending a corner of the tent, which had become torn in packing. Randy was beside him and uttered a cry when he beheld the two men from Basco.

"Tom Roland and Jasper Guardley!" he whispered to his uncle. "Those are the fellows we thought got that money on a false identification!"

"Is that so?" returned Foster Portney. "What can Earl be bringing them here for?"

"This is Mr. Portney, I take it," said Guardley, after clearing his throat awkwardly. "I was thinking—"

"He and his friend want to join us," put in Earl. "I told them that our party was complete."

"Hullo, Randy!" broke in Roland, carelessly. "You'd like us to come into your crowd, wouldn't you?"

Randy was staggered at the request, coming so unexpectedly. He glanced at Earl before replying. "No, I guess not," he said.

"Why, what's the matter with you?" cried Roland, half angrily. "We are all Maine folks, and friends ought to stick together, seems to me."

He turned to Foster Portney and introduced himself and Guardley, and stated his case, adding that he and his companion only wanted to join some party until Dawson City was reached. Mr. Portney listened quietly, and then turned to Captain Zoss, who stood near.

"I don't believe we want any more in our crowd, do you?"

"I reckon we've got a-plenty," was the captain's answer. "Still, if they are friends to the boys—"

"But they are not," whispered Earl. "And what is more, we consider them doubtful characters."

"Then we don't want 'em, nohow."

"This camp is full," came from inside, where Dr. Barwaithe sat, examining his sore foot, which was neither better nor worse. "That boat we are building won't hold more than five people, along with our outfits."

The faces of both Roland and Guardley grew dark. "All right; if you don't want us, we'll hook fast somewhere else," muttered Roland, and turned on his heel.

"Maybe you'll regret throwing us off some day," came from Guardley, as he passed Earl; and then the two men were lost to sight among the tents up the lake shore.

"Oh, what cheek!" burst from Randy, when they were gone. "I wouldn't have Roland in the party for a farm."

"I'd be afraid of Guardley's stealing everything we had," said Earl. "As if we didn't know his real character, and that he had been up before Judge Dobson lots of times!"

"I reckon they'll stand watching, especially that last cur — from what he said to Randy," said Captain Zoss. "He's got a bad eye, he has, eh?"

All hands slept soundly after their hard day's work in the timber, and it was not until they heard others stirring in the morning that they arose. As he was not working on the boat, Dr. Barwaithe took it upon himself to perform the "household duties," as he expressed it, and soon a well-cooked breakfast was arranged on a rude table Captain Zoss had stuck up. The doctor was an excellent cook, and Foster Portney could not help but ask him whence his knowledge had been derived.

"It's easily explained," said the doctor. "I have an older sister who was once the head of a cooking school in Montreal. She insisted on it that every one should know how to cook, especially a bachelor like myself, and she used to deliver her lectures to me, at home, before delivering them at the school. I believe I was an apt pupil, but I never dreamed at that time of how useful the knowledge would become."

"Which goes for to prove a feller can't know too much," remarked Captain Zoss. "But come on," he added, draining off his big tin cup of coffee, and springing up. "That ere boat ain't going to build itself." And off he hurried for the woods, carrying all of the tools he could carry. In a moment the boys and Foster Portney followed him.

They found the rough slabs of lumber as they had left them, and sticking them up in convenient places, began the task of smoothing them off into boards, working first with their axes and then with the drawing-knife and the plane. It was no light labor, and night was again upon them by the time the boards were ready and hauled to the edge of the lake. After supper Foster Portney brought out a measuring-rule and marked off the different parts of the boat, which was to be a flat-bottom affair, with a blunt stern and rather a long-pointed bow.

Another day at Lake Linderman saw the craft put together, false bottom, seats, and all. It was a clumsy affair, and they were glad that they had enough oakum and pitch along to make her fairly water-tight. The other parties in camp were also boat-building, and the scene in the clear and fairly warm weather was a busy one.

Randy had cut down a small, straight tree for a mast, and this was easily set in place and held by guards running across from one gunwale to another. The yard and the boom of this mast were primitive affairs, to be put up whenever desired.

As soon as the pitch had hardened, preparations for leaving the camp were made. All the goods and tools were packed up into the smallest possible space, and stored on board of the *Wild Goose*, as Randy had christened the craft, the eatables, clothing, and blankets being placed on top, so as not to be injured by the water which might get in. The last thing to be taken down was the tent, the fly of which was then adjusted for a sail.

"All aboard!" cried Randy, as he leaped into the bow, with Earl behind him. Captain Zoss followed them, to help keep a lookout ahead, while Mr. Portney and Dr. Barwaithe took places in the stern, one to manage the rudder and the other with an oar ready for use, should they run upon a bar or mud-flat.

Lake Linderman is but a few miles long, lying in the midst of snow-clad mountains, similar to those left behind, although not quite so high. At its lower end it connects with Lake Bennett by a short river where are situated the Homan Rapids. These rapids are among the most dangerous encountered in sailing along the headwaters of the Yukon, and are feared more by some miners than are the famous White Horse Rapids, which the party must pass through later on. To avoid the Homan Rapids many miners travelled straight from Chilkoot Pass to Lake Bennett before stopping to build their boats.

But it was all new territory to our party, for even Foster Portney, in his previous trip to Alaska, had not passed in this direction. A stiff breeze sent them on their way down Lake Linderman, and all expressed themselves as well satisfied with the sailing qualities of the *Wild Goose*.

"We're coming to the end of the lake," observed Earl, when scarcely an hour had passed. "There is the river, over to the right."

In a few minutes more the sail was lowered, and they came to anchor at the mouth of the river. The water at this point was smooth enough, but some distance

"THE WATER WAS BOILING ON EVERY SIDE." — *Page 125.*

ahead could be seen the leaping and swirling whitecaps of the rapids leading to the lake below.

"I reckon we'll have to take a line ashore and haul her through," observed Captain Zoss, after an examination of the situation. "We don't want to run no risk of bein' upsot so early in the game."

This was agreed to, and the captain and Dr. Barwaithe took one line to the left shore and Foster Portney and Randy another to the right, leaving Earl to steer or use the rudder, as might be best.

Some loose ice, floating along the lake shores, had partly choked the stream, but there was a clear place near the centre, and into this the *Wild Goose* drifted. It was not long before she was caught in the strong current, which sent the ice cakes crunching and banging along her sides and the spray flying up into Earl's face. He had started to use the rudder, but now saw this was useless, and sprang forward with the long oar.

"Steady to the left! Not to the right! Swing her around a bit, you fellows over there! Easy now, easy! Shove off from that rock, Earl! Now then, let her down a few feet! That was a narrow shave, boys! There you go again! Steady now! steady! steady!"

So the cries and directions ran on, as the boat proceeded on her perilous voyage. The water was boiling on every side, and the lines which held the craft were as tight as whipcords. Considerable water had been shipped, and Earl was wet from head to foot. But he kept his place and shoved off, this way and that, with might and main.

"Hold hard!" suddenly shouted Foster Portney. "Look out, Earl; the line is going to break!"

The words were hardly spoken when snap! went the line, the boat end hitting Earl a sharp crack in the neck. Thus released, the *Wild Goose* swung around and made straight for a series of rocks which all had been working hard to avoid. Should she strike she would become a total wreck, beyond a doubt, and all their outfits would be lost.

CHAPTER XVI.

AN EXCITING NIGHT IN CAMP.

WHEN the line parted, Foster Portney and Randy were thrown flat on their backs in the six inches of slush and water in which they had been wading along the edge of the rapids. But they did not care for this, the one thought of both was of Earl and how the boat would fare now that there was only one line by which to guide her.

As for Earl, the shock also caused him to lose his balance, and he went down heavily on one of the packs with which the *Wild Goose* was freighted. But he recovered instantly, and sprang to the bow, oar in hand. The craft had swung around, as has been related, and was on the point of smashing on the rocks when he put out the oar and tried to sheer off.

"Hold her! hold her!" roared Captain Zoss to Earl. "Take the line, but don't pull!" he added to the doctor, and the next instant he was in the icy water up to his waist. He could not reach the bow of the boat, but he gained the stern, and catching hold of the rudder he swung the *Wild Goose* in toward a rock and held her there.

"Throw the broken line to Earl and let him tie it, quick!" he shouted to Foster Portney; but the broken line was floating amid the loose ice, and it was several seconds before it could be secured. In that time the current again caught the boat from another direction, and sheering along the rocks in front, the craft made a wild plunge ahead and downward, dragging the captain in her wake.

"Earl will be killed!" groaned Randy, and his heart leaped into his throat as the *Wild Goose* seemed swallowed up in the foaming and boiling waters below them. His uncle did not reply, but darted out of the water and down the bank of the river as fast as his feet could carry him. Dr. Barwaithe, who had been compelled to let go the line in order to save himself, was also running, and now Randy likewise took to his heels.

Fortunately for Earl he kept his wits about him, even though he realized the great peril he was in. In previous years he had helped raft lumber in Maine during the spring freshets, so that the situation was not such a novel one. But there was a vast difference between steering logs which could not be harmed and navigating a boat loaded with all their possessions, and he felt the responsibility. He clung to the long oar and used it as best he could, whenever the opportunity offered, which was not often.

In less than ten minutes the ride was over and the

Wild Goose shot with a swish into Lake Bennett. By this time Captain Zoss had managed to crawl on board and give Earl a helping hand. The craft had struck a dozen times, twice rather sharply, but beyond a scraping on one side and a slight crack in the bow, which was speedily caulked up, she escaped injury. The two on board ran to one shore, to take Dr. Barwaithe on board, and then stood over to where Mr. Portney and Randy awaited them.

"That was a providential escape!" were Foster Portney's words, when he saw that Earl was safe. "I wouldn't have you run such a risk again for a fortune!"

"And I don't want to run such a risk again," replied Earl, with rather a sickly smile. He was greatly shaken up, and it was a long while before he felt like himself. Randy could hardly keep from hugging his brother because of the escape.

"It was a fool move of ours from the start," said Captain Zoss, speaking plainly, for the icy bath had not improved his temper. "We should have packed our outfits along the river and let the boat take care of herself, with plenty of lines to guide her. I won't stand fer any such move as that ag'in; not much, eh?"

"You are right, captain," said Foster Portney, gravely. "We'll be more cautious in the future."

"Yes! yes!" broke in the doctor. "What should we have done had this young man been killed and all our traps been lost? It would have been better to have carried boat and all around from one lake to the next."

It was a sober party which went into camp that night on the rather rocky shore of Lake Bennett, sober and rather out of sorts in the bargain. The captain insisted on building an immense fire, and while he sat drying himself by it he found fault with everything which came into view. Later on the others of the crowd found that the captain got these moods every once in a while and never meant all he said, but now they did not know this and it made the two boys, at least, unhappy.

"Might have knowed it," grumbled Captain Zoss, "with two kids along, instead o' nothing but growed-up men as know their business. The next time I jine a crowd it will be o' those as has at least voted, eh?"

"I can't agree with you that it was the boys' fault," replied Dr. Barwaithe. "The line broke, and that started the whole thing."

"Well, boys is boys, and men wouldn't have let sech a thing happen!" snapped the captain. "See yere, I want my coffee hot!" he roared to Randy, who was preparing supper. "No lukewarm dishwater fer me, eh?"

"I'll give it to you as hot as the fire will make it; I can't do any more," was Randy's short answer. He was as much out of sorts as any one. Then the captain turned to Earl, and found fault with the timber in the boat; and by the time they sat down to eat, all felt thoroughly put out.

The doctor tried to enliven matters by relating some of his experiences in college, and he even gave them a song or two, for he was a good singer with a sweet tenor voice. All enjoyed the singing, but the captain looked as glum as ever.

"I'm sorry we've got that old curmudgeon along," said Earl, as he and Randy turned in together, on the rubber blanket. "Gracious, I never imagined he could be so disagreeable!"

"Nor I," grumbled his brother. "And to think that we have got to put up with him until we reach the gold diggings!"

The tent had been pitched in the shelter of a number of high rocks and at some distance from the lake front. The *Wild Goose* rested in a tiny cove, secured by a painter attached to a stake driven deeply into the sandy shore. There was a little swell on the water, caused by the rising wind, but no one supposed this would prove sufficient to do the craft any harm.

As they expected to remain in that camp but one night only, a single tent had been erected for the entire party, so all hands were huddled closely together. It was not long before they were all asleep.

When Earl awoke it was still dark. He roused up with a start, to find the wind blowing violently. Outside it was raining and snowing together, and it was some snow on his face which had caused him to awake. He was about to get up, when Randy called to him.

"What's up?"

"There's a storm on, snow and rain, and I guess we'll have to look to the fastenings of the tent," answered Earl.

The talking awoke the others. The wind was increasing rapidly, and already the front left end of the tent was flapping violently, torn loose from its pegging. Earl donned his overcoat and ran outside to hold it down, while he called to Randy to bring the hammer with which to bury the pegs anew.

"Fasten her tight; I'll take a look after the boat!" cried Captain Zoss, and rushed off in the darkness, followed by Foster Portney. By this time the doctor was also out, and he and the boys began the task of securing the shelter. A heavy gust of wind came on, and in a flash the canvas was sailing high in the air, held down only by the pegs on one side. To secure the cloth was no mean work, and they had to wait for fully a minute in the rain and snow, until the wind abated.

"This is going to the gold diggings with a vengeance," murmured Dr. Barwaithe.

"A fellow could 'most fly there in this wind!" panted Randy. "Earl, have you a peg handy?"

"Not a one."

"Neither have I, and it's as dark as pitch."

"Here are two pegs," said the doctor. "I wonder if I can stir up that fire," he added, starting to where the campfire had been. The fire was out, and the sheet-iron stove lay over on its side, with a mess of beans overturned in the oven. To light a new fire under existing circumstances was out of the question, and the medical man went back to assist the boys.

The tent had hardly been secured when there came a great flurry of snow which almost blinded them. Randy had been for running down to the lake, but now he crawled under the canvas and hesitated. In the meantime Dr. Barwaithe set the stove up once more and tried to rescue such of the beans as were worth it.

"The rain is giving way to snow—" began Earl, when he stopped short, as a faint shout reached them through the whistling wind. "It's Uncle's voice! We are wanted down there!" he added, and started off on a run. As the cry was repeated Randy followed. A minute's run and they reached the beach a hundred feet above where Captain Zoss and Foster Portney were standing.

"What's the matter?" demanded Earl, quickly.

"The boat is gone," was his uncle's alarming reply. "She has drifted off in the storm, and we can't catch sight of her anywhere!"

CHAPTER XVII.

A HUNT FOR FOOD.

RANDY and Earl were much dismayed by their uncle's announcement. The *Wild Goose* had disappeared! Where to? Ah, that was the question. In vain they tried to pierce the darkness of the night and the snow-squall. Nothing in the shape of a craft could be discerned upon the broad waters of Lake Bennett.

"I told ye to mind how ye tied up that yere craft," growled Captain Zoss, wrathfully, to Earl. "Any lubber could have tied her up better than you did."

"You expect me to do everything!" retorted Earl, beginning to lose his temper, too. "I did the best I could. Why didn't you look after it?"

"He was too busy taking it easy by the fire," put in Randy, bound to stand up for his brother, as well as to put in a "shot" for himself.

"None o' your impudence, boy!" roared the captain, and he turned as if to strike Randy. But now Foster Portney caught his arm and threw it back.

"Stop it, all of you!" said he. "This is no time to

quarrel. The wind, and not Earl, is responsible for this, for I looked to the tying up myself, after he was done. We're all out of sorts, but we needn't act like children over it. Our duty is to find the boat, and that as quickly as possible."

"I reckon she's gone down the lake," grumbled the captain, after an awkward pause. "The wind's that way."

"We'll go down and see if we can't sight her," answered Foster Portney.

Away they went on a run. Earl, who was tall and light in weight, easily outdistanced the rest and reached a rocky cliff, where the lake made a slight bend. He went up the cliff, to stumble headlong into a narrow gulch, cutting his chin and his left hand. Picking himself up, he started on, but soon stopped. "I ought to warn the others," was his thought, and he turned and hurried back.

Captain Zoss was ahead of the others and was on top of the cliff when Earl shouted to him. "Stop, captain, stop, or you'll get hurt!" came at the top of his voice, and the captain halted just in time to save himself from a disastrous fall. He climbed down the gulch and up at the other side, and yelled a warning to those behind. Soon all four stood upon another level stretch of the lake shore.

Nothing was to be seen — that is, nothing but the flying snowflakes dropping into the wind-swept and white-capped waters beneath. They continued to walk on, until the cold chilled each to the marrow of his bones.

"We might as well get back and wait till morning," said Foster Portney, with a heavy sigh. "We can do nothing in the darkness. Let us hope the boat will beach herself somewhere and remain right-side up."

With chattering teeth they started on the return, Randy by his uncle's side and Earl behind Captain Zoss. Half the distance to the tent had been covered when the captain paused and ranged up beside Earl.

"Earl, you mustn't mind me when I git in my tantrums," he said jerkily. "I git 'em every once in a while, see? It's nateral with me — allers was. But I ain't bad at heart, an' I shan't forgit ye for savin' me a dirty fall, mark that! And it's not your fault the boat is gone — anything would have torn loose in this yere gale." He paused for a moment. "An' I didn't mean ter hit Randy — it's only a way I have ter frighten folks — a poor way, too, as I acknowledge. Come on." And before Earl could reply he was stalking on, his head bent far down, to keep the snow from his eyes. Earl clung close to him, and from that night he and the captain were better friends than ever. Later on Randy received a like "apology," and when he got to know the captain better voted him "all right, though a bit cranky at times."

Dr. Barwaithe was as dismayed as any of them

had been, when the news was broken to him, but he agreed that nothing was to be accomplished while the darkness and the storm lasted. He had dragged the cooking stove up to the entrance to the tent and was trying to start a fire. Twice the tiny flames had flickered and gone out, but now, fanned vigorously, the wood caught, and soon the stove was red-hot, the top spluttering with the snowflakes which fell upon it. The fire warmed the air in the tent, and for the balance of the night the party rested comfortably in body if not in mind.

With the coming of morning the storm abated, and by eight o'clock the sun was struggling to shine through the drifting clouds. The captain, as if to atone for his misdeeds, prepared breakfast, giving to Earl and Randy the best of the flap-jacks turned out. The captain was a great hand at these cakes, and the party was certain to get them whenever he was cook.

"For all we know, the boat may have gone clear down to the entrance to Tagish Lake," remarked Foster Portney, while finishing the repast. "I see nothing for us to do but to walk along the lake shore and keep our eyes open."

"Shall we take our traps along?" asked the doctor. "I can carry the cook stove if you can divide the rest of the stuff among you."

A short discussion followed, and feeling certain the boat had gone down the lake, if anywhere, it was decided by all hands to pack the outfit and take it along. The packing took some time, and when the start was made the storm had cleared away entirely, leaving the sky as bright as one could wish.

A mile of the shore had been covered when Foster Portney called a halt and directed attention to an object floating in the direction from which they had come. "It's a boat!" he cried, a moment later.

"Our boat?" questioned Randy, eagerly.

"I can't say." Mr. Portney and the others watched the craft with interest. "No, it's not our boat, but another, and there are several people on board."

"Let's hail 'em, and git 'em to search for the *Wild Goose*," said Captain Zoss, and they walked back, and after some trouble succeeded in attracting the attention of the party on the water. There were three men in the boat and a woman, the latter being the same they had met in camp at Lake Linderman. To all the newcomers Foster Portney told his story.

"O' course we'll help you," said the miner who had his wife on board. "One o' you can git aboard here, and we'll cruise around the lake on a hunt. Ain't got room fer more 'n one," he went on; "and say, who's the doctor among ye?"

"I am," responded Dr. Barwaithe.

"Then you might ez well do the trick, fer Lizy here don't feel extry well, an' it will be fair play fer you to give her some medicine, I take it."

"I'll do what I can for her," said the doctor. "But most of my medicines are on board of the lost boat."

"Then we've got ter find her, sure pop, fer Lizy does feel most distressin' like, with a pain in her head an' a crick in her back," went on Wodley, the miner.

The doctor hopped on board, and after a few words more the boat set off in search of the *Wild Goose*, and the hunt from the lake shore was continued. Slowly the forenoon wore away and still nothing was seen of the missing craft. The other boat with the doctor had long since been lost to view up the lake.

It was getting toward supper time when Foster Portney turned to Earl, who, in addition to some of the camping outfit, carried the shot-gun. "I just caught a glance of something on legs up among yonder rocks," he said. "If you can, you might as well knock it over, for it won't be long before all of us will want something to eat."

Earl was glad enough to try his hand at hunting, and turned over his traps to his companions. Soon he was climbing the rocks to which his uncle had pointed. He had not gone over five hundred feet when he beheld a small deer gazing at him in alarm. Before he could draw a bead on the animal the deer was gone behind a neighboring cliff.

Feeling moderately sure that this was the animal his uncle had seen, and that the deer would not go far, but might even come back out of curiosity, Earl began to climb the cliff. A profusion of brush grew among the rocks, and these afforded him a good hand-hold, and he was soon at the top.

Although hemmed in on three sides by mountains, the way to the lake was clear, and looking in that direction he saw, far to the opposite shore, the boat containing Dr. Barwaithe and their newly made friends. He watched the boat for a minute, when a clatter of sharp hoofs on the cliff made him whirl around, just in time to catch a second sight of the deer. His gun came up quick enough now, and the charge took the animal full in the breast.

Struck in this fashion, many an animal would have rolled over dead. But the deer of Alaska, which are growing more scarce every year, are a sturdy lot, and though terribly wounded, this specimen did not drop. Staggering for a brief moment, he turned and then fled in the direction from which he had come.

Earl was amazed, but, determined not to lose his game after such a shot, he hastily reloaded and made after the game. Less than two score of steps brought him almost to the end of the cliff, and he discovered the deer crouched in the shelter of the rocks, its dark eyes glaring angrily. Up came his gun, and the weapon was discharged just as the animal sprang forward. The shot was a glancing one, doing little harm, and the next instant the wounded beast was upon the boy.

CHAPTER XVIII.

ON TO THE WHITE HORSE RAPIDS.

For a brief instant, as the deer rushed upon him, Earl was fairly paralyzed, having had no idea that the wounded animal might attack him. But as those glaring eyes came closer and the antlers were lowered, he realized that something must be done, and leaped to the inner side of the narrow cliff.

Crash! the deer had struck him on the arm. It was a heavy blow, and only the sharp rock to one side of him saved the youth from serious injury. Then, as the animal bounded back for a second attack, Earl shoved out the gun, pressed it at the deer's breast, and sent the beast tumbling from the cliff into the gulch below. It was done so rapidly that the animal had no time to save itself. It went down with a crash and a dull thud, and, looking over the rocks, the boy saw that it lay on its back unable to run off on account of a broken leg. As soon as he could, he reloaded the shot-gun and put his game out of its misery.

"That was a narrow escape, and no fooling!" he half muttered, as he looked about for some place where he might descend to the bottom of the gulch. A quarter of an hour later he had the deer bound on top of a tree branch, and was dragging it toward the lake shore.

"A deer!" cried Randy and Foster Portney, simultaneously, as they caught sight of the prize. "Well, that was well worth going after!" continued the latter.

"You had a narrow escape!" exclaimed Randy, when Earl's story was told. "If you hadn't shoved him over, he would have gored you to death."

It was quite dark by the time they went into camp. The deer was soon cut up, and they dined that evening on the choicest of venison steak. The remainder of the meat was hung up to dry, while a portion of it was thoroughly salted.

In addition to the fire in the camp stove, a big blaze was lit on the shore, that Dr. Barwaithe and the others might be guided hither if they succeeded in finding the *Wild Goose*. But the night wore away without interruption, and by six o'clock the next morning the search for the missing craft was renewed.

"We're most down to Tagish Lake, I reckon," remarked Captain Zoss. "I don't believe the *Wild Goose* could go through, 'ceptin' she was bottom side up and minus our traps, which I don't hope fer, eh?"

The entrance to Tagish Lake was reached, and they were speculating on what to do next, when Randy shouted, "Here they come, and they have the *Wild Goose* in tow!"

His announcement proved correct, and quarter of an hour later Wodley sent his own craft up to the bank with a swish through the water-grass and tundra, or moss, which was now beginning to show itself on every side. The *Wild Goose* was close behind, and they noted with satisfaction that she seemed to be in the same condition as they had left her.

"We found her stuck in the mud on the other side," announced Dr. Barwaithe. "The wind had just sent her along and left her, and the only damage done is to some of the provisions which were soaked by the rain and snow."

"We can be thankful it's not worse," replied Foster Portney. "If she had not turned up, I don't know what we would have done."

Dr. Barwaithe had become well acquainted with the party, and had given Mrs. Wodley some medicine containing a large quantity of quinine, for the woman was suffering from chills and fever, something frequently met with in Alaska.

It did not take long for both parties to haul their boats into Tagish Lake, and once on that broad sheet of water, all sail was set for the six miles of river which connects that body of water with Marsh Lake, called by many Mud Lake, on account of its shallowness and soft bottom.

As they skimmed along, Earl and Randy, under the directions of their uncle, sorted over the provisions, putting aside for immediate use such as would not keep after being wet. This had scarcely been finished when the end of Tagish Lake appeared in sight.

"There is some sort o' a camp ahead," announced Captain Zoss. "Don't look like er miner's strike, either. Injuns, I'll bet!"

The captain was right. The camp was a rude one, consisting of half a dozen huts and dugouts. The Indians numbered about two score, and they were the most disagreeable Randy and Earl had yet beheld. Each was painted from forehead to chin with greasy black and red paint, and all wore filthy skin suits which could be smelt "further than you could see them," according to Randy's notion. The Indians tried to sell them some fish, but the members of the party declined, and pointed to the deer meat. Then one of the Indians begged Earl to let him have the deer's head and antlers for a string of beautiful pike, and the youth made the trade; for although he would have liked to keep the trophy, carrying it up into the gold regions was out of the question. The deer meat had been divided with the Wodley party, and now a similar disposition was made of the fish.

The day was fine, with the wind in the right direction, and soon they came to the end of Marsh Lake, which is fifteen miles long, and heavily fringed on all sides with timber and brush. On several occasions they ran in water so shallow they were in danger of going aground; but the sharp eyes of Captain Zoss saved them, and the second day saw them encamped within sight of the fifty-mile river which connects Marsh Lake with Lake Labarge, the last of the lakes they were to traverse on the way to the gold regions.

"By day after to-morrow we'll strike the White Hoss Rapids," said Captain Zoss. "Then, I reckon we'll have jest sech a time as we had up ter Homan Rapids."

"Excuse me!" rejoined Earl. "One such experience is enough in a lifetime."

"I have been talking to Wedley," put in Foster Portney. "He has been through the rapids, and he says he will give us a hand when we get there. He advises taking the boats through almost empty."

The captain "allowed" this would be safer, although, to be sure, it would also be far more laborious, for everything not left in the boat would have to be carried over the roughest kind of a trail, running some distance away from the stream.

The two parties camped side by side, and it made each feel more at home to have the other at hand, for among these lofty and cold-looking mountains one was very apt to have a lonely feeling creeping over him if no companion were at hand.

"How a man could attempt this trip all alone is

something I can't understand," observed Randy. "Imagine getting lost in those mountains over yonder! It makes a fellow shiver to think of it!"

"Men have been lost out here," replied Dr. Barwaithe, gravely, "and lost so thoroughly they have never been heard of again. If a man gets lost in the mountains, and he is of a nervous temperament, the chances are that after a week or a month of it he will lose his mind and go crazy."

"I guess that is what would happen to me," answered Randy. "Oh, what's that stung me? A mosquito, I declare! Who would expect to find one of those pests at this season of the year?"

"You'll get mosquitoes enough presently," replied Foster Portney. "Don't you remember the mosquito netting I brought along? During the short summer here the insects are apt to worry the life out of a person."

"I suppose they thrive in this moss that I see around," said Earl. "What did you say it was called, Uncle Foster? tundra?"

"Yes, tundra, Earl. The moss is thicker than this up in the north and covers everything. If it wasn't for the moss, I think the ground might thaw out more in the summer, but as it is, the moss prevents the sun from striking in, and the ground is as hard as in midwinter six or eight feet below the surface."

"The moss doesn't seem to have any effect on the

berry bushes, though," said Randy. "I see 'em everywhere. Do they bear fruit?"

"Oh, yes, they have everything in the way of berries up here, Randy. But they are rather small, and they haven't the flavor of those at home. The berries have to take the place of larger fruits, such as apples, pears, and peaches, and the birds live on them."

"Well, we won't starve as long as we have berries, birds, and fish," said Earl. "I don't see where this cry of starvation comes in, I must say."

"O' course ye don't — not now!" burst in Captain Zoss. "But wait till winter sets in. Then the berries will be gone, an' birds will be mighty scarce."

"But we'll have the fish, captain. We can cut holes in the ice on the river and spear them, as we do down in Maine."

"Wall, maybe, my lad. But ye don't catch me a-tryin' it when I kin git anything else — not with the ice eight or ten feet thick an' the mercury down to forty below nuthin' at all!"

It was not long after that they turned in, and never did they sleep more soundly, although a number of mosquitoes visited them. Foster Portney was the first to get up, and by the time the boys followed, a delicious smell of frying fish and boiling coffee was floating through the air.

A ten minutes' ride on the lake brought them close to the entrance of the river. Here the water was broken up into a dozen currents, swirling this way and that and throwing the spray in every direction. On either side of this watercourse were high walls.

"Now fer the tug o' war!" said Captain Zoss, and immediate preparations were made to shoot the cañon and the falls of which Randy and Earl had heard so much. Once past that dangerous spot, the remainder of the trip to the gold regions would be an easy one.

CHAPTER XIX.

NEARING THE END OF A LONG JOURNEY.

Both Earl and Randy had heard from the miner Wodley that it was only of late years that prospectors after gold in Alaska had had the daring to shoot the White Horse Rapids, of which even the Indians in their light canoes were afraid. Formerly white men had packed everything, even to their boats, round the dangerous runs of water, a task which to them looked herculean, when they gazed at the tall mountains, and at the crooked trail Wodley pointed out.

After much talking by all hands, it was decided that Wodley's boat should go through first, loaded down only with the mining tools, which would not suffer from getting wet. Wodley was at first going to take the trip alone, leaving his wife and the other miners of the party to join the Portney crowd, but at the last moment Captain Zoss asked to be allowed to take a hand, and the offer was accepted.

The sail was taken from the *Buster*, as Wodley had named his craft, a heavy-set affair, built to stand some rough usage, and, each armed with an oar and a heavy pole, the two men shoved off from the rocky shore. A few strokes sufficed to send them into the current, and fairly caught, the boat swung around and started on her mad career through the cañon of rocks and water and flying spray.

"She's off!" shouted Earl, and followed by Randy he sped alongshore and up to the edge of the cañon, where he might see what progress was made. But hardly had they reached a convenient spot when the *Buster* shot along far beneath them, and around a bend, and was hidden from view in the midst of a whirlpool of waters that threatened each instant to ingulf her.

"If she isn't smashed up before she reaches the end of the cañon, then I'll miss my guess!" ejaculated Earl. "My, but how she did spin along!"

"Wodley ought to know what he's doing," answered Randy. "If she is smashed up, I hope he and the captain come out alive."

They returned to where the others had been left, and took up the heavy packs which had been assigned to them. All the things to be carried had been equally divided among the men and the boys, and it was calculated that three trips would be necessary to move the outfits.

That day proved the hardest they had yet experienced, and by the time it was dark both Randy and Earl felt as if their backs were broken and their feet, to use Earl's expression, "walked off." They had carried one-third of their traps to a beautiful spot just at the head of the worst of the White Horse Rapids, which, it may be well to add here, are many miles in extent.

Contrary to the expectation of the boys, Wodley and Captain Zoss had brought the *Buster* through in safety. They had had only one alarm, just at the end of the cañon proper, when the boat had swung around on a hidden rock and shipped about half a barrel of water. They were wet to the skin, and this, along with the story they told, made Mrs. Wodley insist upon it that her husband allow the other men of the party to bring the *Wild Goose* through, on the day following.

As Captain Zoss had made the trip once, it was decided that he and Earl should take the next trip, while the others made another tramp over the trail with more of the traps. They encamped at the White Horse Rapids, but started back toward Lake Marsh before sunrise.

"It's easy enough, Earl," said the captain, on embarking on the *Wild Goose*. "All you've got to do is to keep your wits about you and your eyes on the rocks. Tie the pail fast to the seat, so it won't float away if the boat gives too much of a lurch. If we have to bail any, you had better do it."

They were soon on the way, out of the brightness of the early sunshine into the gloom of the yawning cañon, which seemed to swallow them up. The roar of the waters between the rocks was deafening, and the flying spray sent a shiver through Earl. Yet he stood to his post manfully, realizing that there was no turning back, now that the perilous trip was once begun.

"To the left shore!" roared Captain Zoss, presently, and Earl scarcely heard him. The captain waved his elbow frantically, while using his pole, and Earl saw what was wanted. They were running close to some half-submerged rocks. A vigorous use of the pole, a slight grating which made the youth hold his breath, and that danger at least was past.

But more were ahead, and they grew thicker and thicker as the *Wild Goose* leaped, turned, and twisted, first in one mad current and then another. Swish! came a huge wave into the craft, nearly taking Earl from his feet. Then, before he could make up his mind whether to begin bailing or not, the boat slid up almost on her stern's end, and most of the water went flying forth. "Now for the left shore, and mind the channel!" roared the captain, once more, and then the oars came into play, and on they bounded through a clear cut in the rocks not over twenty-five feet wide. The cut at an end, the captain threw down his oar with a deep breath of satisfaction.

"The wust on it's over," he announced. "Jest pole her along easy-like now, and we'll be down to camp inside of half an hour."

The strain on the *Wild Goose* had caused several of the seams to part, but it was decided to do nothing with these until after the worst of the White Horse Rapids had been passed. They must now take their crafts out of water and carry or ride them on rollers to the foot of the falls.

This was a job lasting several days, for both the *Wild Goose* and the *Buster* were heavy, and it took all the men in both parties to move one boat at a time. But at last the greatest of the falls was passed, and then it was decided to draw the boats along through what remained, and after another hard day's labor they had the satisfaction of finding themselves free from further obstacles, and encamped midway between Tahkheena River and the head of Lake Labarge. That day was Sunday, and it was spent in perfect rest by all.

Thus far since the snow-squall on Lake Bennett, fine weather had favored them, but now Monday set in cloudy and threatening. As soon as breakfast was over, the *Wild Goose* was patched up and pitched over, and all of the outfit placed on board. The *Buster* was already loaded, and with the wind from the westward they tacked down the river and into Lake Labarge, a clear sheet of water, some twenty odd miles in length, and varying from two to four miles in width. About midway from either end of the lake there was an island, and on this rocky shore they were compelled to seek shelter about the middle of the afternoon, for the wind had increased to a good-sized blow, and to sail in such a boat was, consequently, out of the question.

Both the *Wild Goose* and the *Buster* had hardly been drawn up out of harm's way than it began to rain. Seeing this, all lost no time in pitching the tents and in building fires to keep warm, for in this section of Alaska a rain even in the summer is sure to make one feel cold. The tents were pegged down with extra care, and this was a good thing, for by nightfall the wind had increased to a hurricane.

The travellers to the gold regions were stormbound at Lake Labarge for two days. It did not rain all this time, but the wind blew too strongly to venture from shore. The time was spent inside the tent and hung rather heavily, although occasionally relieved by a song from the doctor, or a yarn told by Captain Zoss, or Wodley, who, along with his wife, and Crimmins and Johnson, the other two miners, made themselves quite at home with the Portney party.

"The wind has moderated at last!" said Randy, who was the first out on the third morning. "Now let us make the most of the fine weather while it lasts."

The others were more than willing, and the stove and camping outfit were taken down to the *Wild Goose* without delay. The Wodley party was also stirring, but did not start until some time later on; and the two parties did not see each other again until many a day later.

The journey to the end of Lake Labarge was quickly made, and they entered the thirty-mile watercourse, at that time unnamed, which connects the lake with the Big Salmon and the Lewes rivers. Randy and Earl were in charge, the men taking it easy over their pipes, for the captain was an inveterate smoker, and Mr. Portney and the doctor indulged occasionally in the weed.

A good many miles had been covered, when Earl, happening to glance at his pocket compass, announced that they were sailing almost due southward. "And that can't be right," he said to Randy. "We ought to be headed for the northwest."

"Well, we're on the river all right," answered Randy. Nevertheless, he spoke to his uncle about it, who at once consulted his pocket map.

"I'll tell you what you've done," he announced presently. "Instead of sticking to the river that flows northward, you have turned into the Teslin, which flows to the south. Swing the *Wild Goose* around at once."

Much crestfallen over their mistake, the boys did as requested. They had to go back nearly four miles, as they calculated, before they saw the opening which had previously escaped their notice. But once right, they found the wind directly in their favor, and with the sail set to its fullest, they bowled along until the Big Salmon was reached, and they swept into the broad waters of the Lewes River.

"And now for the Yukon and the gold regions!" cried Dr. Barwaithe. "How much further have we to go?" he questioned, turning to Foster Portney.

"About three hundred and fifty miles," was the answer. "And with the exception of the Rink and Five Finger rapids, which don't amount to much, so I have heard, we'll have straight sailing. Ten days more ought to see us at Dawson City, ready to stake our claims."

CHAPTER XX.

THE GOLD FIELDS AT LAST.

On the following day the wind died down utterly, and no progress could be made in the *Wild Goose* excepting by the use of oars, and this was slow and laborious work. They took turns at rowing, two at a turn, with the others taking it easy on the blankets, for the river was now broad and deep and as smooth as a millpond.

On the second day they seemed to leave the rocks behind, and emerged into a slightly hilly country. Here the banks of the stream were overgrown with bushes and flowers, the latter just starting to push forth their buds in countless profusion of variety and color. The transformation was almost magical and more than one spoke of it.

"That's the way of things in Alaska," said Foster Portney. "There are no spring and autumn; just winter and summer, and that's all. The warm weather which is now coming on will last until September, and then winter will come almost before you know it."

Earl had noticed the increase in heat since leaving

the lakes, and now he perspired freely while pulling at the long oar. Randy sat in the bow taking in the sights. A flock of wild geese came sweeping toward them, and he asked for permission to take a shot with the gun. His aim was a good one, and two of the creatures fell where they were readily picked up.

"We'll have stuffed goose to-night," said the captain, with a grin. "It's a pity we ain't got sage an' onions ter stuff it with."

"Perhaps I can find something to take the place of sage," said the doctor. "This variety of bushes and vines ought to produce some similar herb."

During the past two days they had noted a number of islands in the river, and that night they made a landing on one of these, in preference to tying up on shore. Mosquitoes were more numerous than ever, but a smudge built by Foster Portney soon drove the most of the insects off.

The island was several acres in extent, and while the captain busied himself in roasting a goose and frying some potatoes he had "traded in" from Wodley for a bit of bacon, Randy and Earl took a tramp around, to stretch their legs and prospect on the sly. One carried a pick and a shovel and the other a gold-washing pan, and coming to a hollow where they could work unobserved, they set about getting out some dirt from under a series of rocks. The pan was soon full, and then Earl started to wash by pouring water on top and giving it the rotary motion he had heard his uncle mention.

The labor was harder than either of them had imagined, and four panfuls of dirt were washed out, leaving nothing but smooth stones behind. They were about to continue the process, when they heard their uncle calling them, and a moment later Foster Portney appeared. He started to laugh, but quickly checked himself.

"Digging for gold, eh?" he said. "Well, I don't think you'll find any here. The formation of the ground isn't right. If there is any precious metal around at all, it's at the bottom of yonder river. Might as well give it up." And somewhat disgusted the boys returned to camp. It was the only time they tried prospecting until the regular gold fields were reached.

Two days later found them at the Rink and Five Finger rapids. Owing to the melting of the snow and ice under the increasing heat of the sun, the river was very high now, and, consequently, both spots were passed with comparative ease, the dangerous rocks being covered to a depth of a yard or more. In consequence of this increase of water, the river had overflowed its bank for miles, forming great lakes and marshes everywhere, and at times it was almost impossible for them to keep to the channel. Once they did make a false turn, only to find themselves, half an hour later, in a "blind pocket," as Dr. Barwaithe put it.

The rapids and the Tachun River passed, it was almost a straight sail northwest to the ruins of old Fort Selkirk. But little could be seen of the former fort, the Indians having overturned the very foundations in their search for trinkets and articles of value. They encamped at the spot over-night and were joined on the following morning by two other parties who had crossed Chilkoot Pass two days after themselves.

Of these parties Earl asked for news of Tom Roland and Jasper Guardley, and was informed that the men had joined a crowd of Irishmen from Portland, who were coming through on a large raft. "They're a tough crowd, too — all of 'em," said the speaker. "If they don't get into trouble before they leave the gold diggings, it will be mighty queer."

From old Fort Selkirk to Dawson City is a distance of one hundred and sixty miles, through a country so varied that it is next to impossible to describe it. At times the voyagers found themselves sailing calmly along on a broad expanse of water dotted here and there with wooded islands, rich in new foliage and evergreen trees, and again the stream would narrow, with high and rocky hills on either side. Here the water would flow swiftly over and around jagged rocks, and the utmost care would have to be exercised in avoiding a smash-up. Once they did receive a severe shaking-up and had to run for a low island with all possible speed, to avoid becoming waterlogged. This happened in the forenoon, and it took the balance of the day to make the *Wild Goose* as seaworthy as before.

A week and more had slipped by since leaving the Rink Rapids, and now all were on the watch for the first sight of the new gold fields. Every one was in a state of suppressed excitement. They had met half a dozen miners sailing back and forth on the river and from these had learned that everything was "booming," and that strikes were panning out big. The eyes of both Randy and Earl glistened when they heard these stories, and the hardships endured since leaving Dyea were forgotten.

"Hurrah! there's a miner's tent!" suddenly shouted Randy, late one afternoon. "We've struck the diggings at last!"

"There are half a dozen tents and a board cabin!" added Earl, pointing still further on. "I guess you're right, Randy. I wonder if that is the Klondike River over yonder. It looks mighty small."

"That's only a creek," said Foster Portney. "We'll land and see how far we are from Dawson."

The *Wild Goose* was easily beached, and they lost no time in hunting up the miners to whom the tents and the cabin belonged. They were a party of Frenchmen from Canada and could speak but little English. Dr. Barwaithe spoke to them in their native tongue and soon learned that the place was Baker's Creek and that Dawson City was about six miles further on. The

Frenchmen were very conservative, but admitted that they were doing very well at placer-mining, taking out an average of thirty dollars a day per man.

"Thirty dollars a day!" cried Randy. "A fellow can get rich quick enough at that rate."

"Hardly — with such a short season," answered his uncle. "Yet thirty dollars isn't bad by any means."

"I'm up yere to strike a fortune," put in the captain. "No measly little thirty dollars a day fer me!"

Both Randy and Earl wished to remain behind to see the Frenchmen wash out the gold dust, but the others were impatient to go on, and they were soon on the way once more.

"If the claims are good around here, it won't be long before they are taken up," said Foster Portney. "For, as you can see, men are pouring in over the mountains every day, not to say anything of those who make the long trip by way of the ocean and up the Yukon."

"Well, I'm just crazy to get to work," declared Randy. "Just think of the gold lying around ready to be picked up!"

His uncle smiled. Poor Randy! Little did he dream of the many backaches and privations in store for him.

To the left of the river there now arose a long chain of hills and mountains, sloping gradually to the water's edge; on the right were smaller hills and great marshes, fairly choked with bushes and wild growths of vines

THE GOLD FIELDS AT LAST.

and flowers. The tundra was everywhere, and over all circled flocks and flocks of wild birds, a few mosquitoes, and something they had not yet seen — horseflies. The horseflies were black and green in color, and a bite from one of them made Captain Zoss utter a mighty yell of pain. "It was like the stab of a dagger!" he declared afterwards, and so angry did the bite become, and so painful, that the doctor was called upon to treat it with a soothing lotion.

It was after seven o'clock, but still daylight, when Dr. Barwaithe raised his hand for the others to become silent. "Listen!" he said. "I think I heard a steamboat whistle. Ah! I was right. A boat is on the river!"

A few minutes passed, and they heard the whistle again. Then Earl pointed ahead excitedly. "There's the boat, and she is tied up to the river bank. There are half a dozen buildings and fifty tents or more. I'll wager it's Dawson!"

With hearts which beat quickly they sailed forward, using the oars to make the *Wild Goose* move the faster. Another turn of the stream and the mining town could be seen quite plainly. Ten minutes later they ran up just behind the steamboat and tied fast. The long trip was at an end. The new diggings, with all their golden hopes, lay before them.

CHAPTER XXI.

A DAY IN DAWSON CITY.

At the time of which I write, Dawson City was little better than a rude mining camp, containing, as has been previously mentioned, a half dozen board buildings and fifty tents, strung along what was known as the principal "street." Back in the timber land a rude saw-mill had been set up, and this was beginning to get out lumber at the moderate price of one hundred and twenty-five dollars per thousand feet!

A year before Dawson City had been unknown, but the rich finds of gold on Bonanza and Gold Bottom creeks had caused the miners to leave Circle City and Forty Mile Post and boom the new El Dorado, as it was termed, and the settlement grew as if by magic. From the wild rush to stake claims many rows resulted, but the cooler heads speedily took matters in hand, and each man was allowed a claim from five to fifteen hundred feet long and extending the width of the creek or gulch in which it was located.

These claims were not located upon the Klondike River, which joins the Yukon at Dawson City, as has been often supposed, but upon the little watercourses running into the Klondike. These gold-bearing diggings are, or were, variously called Bonanza, Gold Bottom, and Bear creeks, which flow into the Klondike direct, and Hunker, Last Chance, El Dorado, Adams, Shantantay, and other creeks and semi-wet gulches which are tributaries to the creeks first named. The names were arbitrary, and were often changed to suit the miners' tastes.

To Randy and Earl, the camp presented the appearance of having "just moved in," as the younger brother termed it. On every side were miners' outfits stacked in little piles, while their owners were either at hand erecting tents, or off prospecting or buying supplies. There was but one store, a rude board building not over twenty by thirty feet, in which everything on hand was offered at most extravagant prices. Flour sold for sixty dollars per barrel, beans fifty cents per pound, bacon and canned meats seventy-five cents per pound, and other goods in proportion. There were no fresh meats excepting two sides of beef just brought in by the little flat-bottomed steamboat from Circle City, and which were rapidly disposed of at two dollars to five dollars per pound. A crate of eggs were at hand, to be purchased at one dollar per dozen, but as most of the eggs were stale, the contents of the crate went begging. Of miners' tools, a pick or a shovel brought ten dollars to fifteen dollars, while washing pans were not to be found, and had to be manufactured by the miners themselves. Wearing apparel was also scarce, and Earl saw twenty dollars given for a flannel shirt, and five dollars for a pair of socks, both articles being paid for in gold dust.

As it was evening, most of the miners had given up work and come into the camp to talk, trade, and learn the latest news. Every one was in a quiver of excitement, and the announcement that an extra good find had been made on Hunker Creek caused many to strike out during the night to make new claims in that vicinity.

"Let us go, too!" cried Randy, and Earl joined in; but the men talked it over and decided to remain in Dawson City until they learned more about the "lay of the land." They pitched their tent as close to where their boat lay as possible, but it is doubtful if any of the party slept through that short night, which had hardly anything of darkness.

All told, there were not over six hundred white men in camp, and, in addition, there were perhaps a hundred Indians, with their squaws, children, and dogs; for no Alaskan Indian family is complete without from one to a half-dozen canines attached. The Indians were there to sell fish and game, and to pick up odd jobs of pack-carrying. They took but little interest in the gold strikes, and it was but rarely that they could be found mining, and then never for themselves.

One of the first lessons to be learned by the boys and the others, was that of keeping their outfits intact.

Hardly were they up in the morning than a dozen miners and prospectors came shuffling around offering them various prices for this and that. Had they been willing to sell, they could have disposed of all they possessed by noon, but, cautioned by Foster Portney, they were firm, and nothing was allowed to change hands but a small bottle of cough syrup which the doctor sold for an ounce of gold, worth sixteen dollars, to a poor fellow suffering with a slight attack of pneumonia. The doctor wanted no pay, but the miner insisted on giving it, saying he would pay a thousand dollars if the physician would make him as well and strong as ever again.

After many careful inquiries, it was decided that the party should first try its luck on Gold Bottom Creek, at some spot near to where the watercourse was joined by Hunker and Last Chance creeks. They had learned that while Bonanza and El Dorado creeks were paying well, all the best claims in those localities were already staked out.

Two days later found them encamped at the entrance to a tiny watercourse, which flowed into Gold Bottom Creek. They had come in from the Klondike with their outfits on their backs and half a dozen Indians to aid them, for the trail was over rough rocks and through lowlands of berry bushes and tundra,—a wearisome walk which to Randy, at least, seemed to have no end. Often they sank up to their knees in the muck and cold water, and once the doctor got "stuck" and had to be hauled forth by main strength and minus one boot, which was afterward recovered. A promising spot was reached by nightfall, the Indians were paid and sent off, and they set about making themselves a home, temporary or permanent, as fortune might elect.

A flat surface on the side of a small hill was selected, and the tents were placed end to end, as before, but tightened down to stay. Then a trench was dug around the sides and the back, so that when it rained the water might drain off. This done, the interior was carpeted with small branches of pine and evergreen.

"A good, healthful smell," said the doctor, referring to the greens; "and one that will ward off many a cold. On the top of those branches one ought to sleep almost as comfortably as on a feather bed."

The interior of the tents arranged, a fireplace was next in order, a semicircular affair of stone, in which the sheet-iron stove might be sheltered from the wind. Then came a cache for the provisions to be stored away; and their domestic arrangements were complete.

It was bright and early on the day following that all hands set off to prospect along the bottom of the gulch, which the boys had named Prosper. They were divided into two parties, the doctor and the captain in one, and the boys and their uncle in the other. The latter turned up to the left arm of the gulch and presently came to a little hollow, where the tiny stream of water flowing along had deposited some coarse sand to a depth of eight to twenty inches.

"Now we'll shovel up some of this sand in the pan and see what it amounts to," said Foster Portney. "Don't take what is right on top, boys. If there is any gold, it is down next to the bed rock. And don't fill the pan too full." The boys worked eagerly, and soon had the pan nearly full of the sand. Mr. Portney then carried it to a nearby pool and allowed the water to run over the top, then brushed off the surface and began to "wash down." This took several minutes, and Randy and Earl stood by almost breathless during the process.

At last only a handful of sand and dirt remained at the bottom of the pan. All three examined it with care. Here and there could be seen a tiny grain of dull yellow.

"That is gold," explained Foster Portney. "But there is hardly enough to pay; probably three or four cents' worth in all."

"Is that all!" cried Randy, and his voice was full of disappointment. Earl said nothing, but gathered up the pick and shovel and moved on.

In two days a dozen other spots had been tried with even worse success, and the three in the party began to imagine that the gulch was of no consequence, so far as staking a claim there was concerned. To add to their discomfiture a miner came along who said he had gone all over that locality a month previous.

"Ain't nothin' thar," he announced; "nothin' wuth

over four or five cents a panful. Better try your luck elsewar, friends."

"We'll put in another day over here," announced Foster Portney. "One day won't count very much, and ground is often gone over a dozen times before the right strike is made."

They had brought a lunch with them, and now sat down on the edge of a small stony cliff to eat it. The boys were tremendously hungry and could have devoured twice as much as what was on hand, but they were beginning to learn that short rations would be something to look forward to for some time to come.

Having eaten what was allotted to him, Randy began to poke around with the pick, while his uncle and Earl still rested. The cliff was divided into two sections, and between was a lot of rotten stone, dirt, muck, and rubbish. Striking the pick deeply into this, Randy loosened a portion of the stone, and out it rolled into the gulch, bringing the dirt and a good portion of the rubbish after it. He began to scatter the stuff to the right and the left when something shiny caught his eye, and stooping he picked it up, while his heart leaped into his throat.

"Uncle Foster! Earl! Look at this!" he cried, and ran to them, holding up the object as he did so. It was larger than an egg and quite heavy. Foster Portney gave one glance and then leaped forward, dropping what food still remained in his hand.

"Where did you find it, Randy?" he exclaimed.

"Over yonder," was the hasty reply. "But is it gold, Uncle Foster?"

"Yes, Randy, it's a nugget as sure as you're born — a nugget worth at least two hundred dollars. And what's better yet," went on Mr. Portney as Randy began to dance with delight, "the chances are that there are more where this came from!"

CHAPTER XXII.

DIGGING FOR GOLD.

A NUGGET worth two hundred dollars! Randy could scarcely believe his eyes and ears. He gazed at his uncle for a moment in open-mouthed wonder.

"You're in luck, and no mistake!" broke in Earl, as he also examined the yellowish lump. "Say, but that's a strike to start on, isn't it!"

He had hoped to make the first find himself, but he was too unselfish to begrudge his brother that pleasure. Leaving the lump in his uncle's possession, Randy led the way back to where the find had been made, and all three set to work without delay to empty the "pocket," as Foster Portney called it, and examine the contents.

"Here's another!" cried Earl, presently. "It's not quite so large, though."

"But it's worth at least a hundred dollars, Earl," answered his uncle. "And see, here are a number of little fellows worth from ten dollars to fifty each. Randy has struck a bonanza beyond a doubt. Don't scatter that dirt too much, for we must wash out every ounce of it for little nuggets and dust."

"And maybe there is a vein of gold back there,"

said Randy, proudly. "If there is, we can all work it, can't we?"

"Yes, unless the captain and the doctor have struck something equally good. There, that seems to be the last of the nuggets. Let us count them. Fourteen in all, and worth at least four hundred dollars. It paid to stay over in spite of what that miner said, didn't it?" And Foster Portney laughed, and the boys joined in readily, for the discovery of so much gold had put all into the best of humor.

The nuggets picked out, they set to work to wash out the sand and dirt. While Foster Portney filled the pan and washed, the two boys took turns in bringing up water from the pool, using for the purpose a rubber water bag the man had thoughtfully provided for just such an emergency. The washings continued until it was quite dark, and by that time half of the dirt had been gone over and something like two ounces of gold dust extracted.

"Not so bad," said Mr. Portney. "Perhaps to-morrow we'll do even better."

"I could keep on all night," declared Randy, who was loath to quit the locality. "Somebody may come in and take the claim away from us before morning."

"We'll leave the pick and the shovel in it, and that will prevent them," was the answer; and this was done. No miner dares to touch another's "prospect" so long as any tools remain in it.

When they got back to camp they found the doctor and the captain already there. The two had tried half a dozen spots, but only one had yielded sufficient gold dust to warrant their continuing to work it. They listened with keen interest to the account of the find made by Randy, and were quite willing to take a hand at prospecting that locality the next day.

Eight o'clock found all hard at work. While the captain and Earl washed, the others went into the opening of the cliff and brought out all that remained of the dirt and loose stones. There was not a great deal, and shortly after noon every shovelful was heaped up close to the artificial pool of water Dr. Barwaithe had constructed. While the washing continued, Foster Portney examined the sides and the bottom of the opening, and then moved forward through a tangled mass of brushwood and tundra until he came to the bed of a second gulch a hundred feet distance from the first.

"There is nothing more in the pocket," he declared. "And if there is any more gold, it is either in that gulch or this, and I am half inclined to think it is over there, although we may as well prospect this gulch thoroughly first."

By the morrow the washings from the pocket came to an end, with four more ounces of gold to the credit of the prospectors, making in all a find of about five hundred dollars. Previous to going into camp it had been decided that for the present everything found should be divided into five parts, one to go to the captain, one to the doctor, and three to Foster Portney for himself and his nephews. The Portney share, as we know, was to be divided, one-half to Mr. Portney and one-quarter to each of the boys. Thus the boys received each three-twentieths of the entire amount found; not a large portion, but then they had nothing to pay out for expenses, which were bound to be considerable, and each was perfectly willing that his uncle should have the one-tenth extra of the whole amount on that account.

"Three-twentieths of five hundred dollars is seventy-five dollars," said Randy to Earl, when they were alone. "We've each earned that, free and clear, so far. That's not bad."

"If only we can continue, we'll make our fortunes." replied Earl, earnestly. "But the pocket's at an end, and now we've got to prospect elsewhere."

The days went by, and they tried the first of the gulches from end to end, sometimes working together, and then each man and boy for himself. But though they struck gold often it was never in paying quantities, and the end of the week saw them somewhat discouraged.

"It wouldn't be so bad, only we made such a fine start," grumbled Randy. "Now there's no telling when we shall find gold again."

"That's the fortunes o' prospectin'," said the captain. "It may be we won't git a smell o' gold in the hull district ag'in!"

"I move we try that other gulch on Monday," put in the doctor. "It's full of loose sand, isn't it?" he went on to Foster Portney.

"Yes, the sand and gravel are at least two feet thick," was the answer. "I believe there is gold there, as I said before, but to clear off the brush and moss will be no easy task."

"We came out here for work," said Earl. "I didn't expect to sit around and sun myself." And all laughed at this remark.

It was Sunday, and late on Saturday night a miner had been around announcing a religious meeting to be held over at the Bottom at noon. Mr. Portney, the boys, and the doctor walked over, nearly half a mile, leaving the captain in charge of the camp. They found about fifty miners collected around an improvised platform, where an earnest-looking young man was reading a chapter from his Bible. A song by three of the women present followed, and then came a short sermon on the brotherhood of man and the value of a faith which would carry a man above the temptation to do wrong, even in that desolate region. At the close of the service a collection was taken up, for the preacher's benefit, some of the miners giving ordinary money, and others pouring gold dust into the little chamois bag the preacher had provided for that purpose.

At this meeting the Portneys again met the Wodley crowd, who had located about a mile up Gold Bottom Creek, at a place called Rosebud, a name particularly inappropriate, since no roses were to be found in the vicinity. Wodley and his companions were doing fairly well, and thought the "doctor's flock" might do worse than to locate just above them.

"We'll remember that," said Foster Portney. "But first we are going to try again over where we are."

Wodley had heard again from Tom Roland and Guardley. He said the gang, as he termed it, which they had joined had gone up Hunker Creek and staked out three claims somewhere above Discovery, as the first claim on a creek or gulch is called. The claims had overlapped some already staked out, and the miners in that section had had several fights and had threatened to drive out all the newcomers if they did not do what was right.

"I was going over to Hunker Creek myself," concluded Wodley. "But I don't want to quarrel with anybody."

Monday morning found the entire Portney crowd over to Tangle Gulch, as Mr. Portney christened it. It was a name well chosen, for the tangle of bushes, vines, and moss was "simply out of sight," so Earl said, although as a matter of fact it was very much in sight — that and nothing else. No one could move forward more than a yard before having to stop to loosen himself, either from the bushes and vines or the clinging moss, and muck under the moss. And to add to their discomfort they stirred up a legion of mosquitoes, gnats, and black flies, which hovered over their heads like a cloud.

"Let us burn the brush first of all," said the doctor, when at last the middle of the gulch was reached. "That will clear the surface and scatter those pests overhead. Oh, my!" He broke off short as he went down into a concealed water hole which was several feet deep. "Here's another of the pleasures of hunting gold in Alaska!" and this was said so comically that everybody roared.

Axes and knives had been brought along, and soon a large pile of the brush had been cut and piled in a heap and set on fire. As it was green, it burnt slowly and raised a large smoke, which made the mosquitoes scatter immediately. From that day until the end of the summer they kept a smudge fire for protection. The brush cleared from the sides of the gulch, which was very narrow, they went at the tundra, throwing the moss wherever it would be out of the way. This took a long time, and it was not until almost nightfall that they got down to the sand and gravel of the choked-up watercourse.

"Now we'll see if there is anything in this gulch or

not," said the captain, as he scooped up the first panful off the bedrock. "If there isn't, then we've had most all-fired hard work fer nuthin', eh?" And he started in to wash up the sand, gravel, and dirt, while the others looked on in breathless interest.

CHAPTER XXIII.

GOOD LUCK AND BAD.

As the captain wanted to save every grain of gold in the pan, he washed very carefully, and it was fully five minutes before the last of the sand and dirt was disposed of and they could come to a calculation as to the value of the yellow metal left.

For gold there was, true enough, shining brightly before their eyes — and there was more than this, too, for some of it was of a blackish color. The others could not believe in the value of this until Foster Portney assured them that he had frequently heard of black gold being turned up in the Yukon district.

"Half an ounce at least," was the verdict arrived at by both the captain and Mr. Portney; "and that's eight dollars."

"Then we had better stay, hadn't we?" said Earl.

"Why, of course, Earl; you didn't expect to do much better than that, unless you struck nuggets."

"One fellow over to Gold Bottom said he was taking out a hundred dollars to the panful," put in Randy.

"Fairy stories, my lad," answered the captain. "A

claim as will turn out eight dollars to the pan is mighty good — as good as I'm a-lookin' fer just now."

"And we haven't gone very far into this gulch," put in the doctor. "It may be better further up."

"And it may be worse," said Foster Portney, "although I'm inclined to think it will be better. We had best stake out our claims without delay."

This was readily agreed to, and before they went back to the tents they had staked out three claims, one for each of the men. Earl might have taken up a claim, too, being just old enough, but the three covered all the ground which the party thought of any account. Each claim was five hundred feet long and the upper one covered both gulches, which was an excellent thing, as it would give them a fair amount of water by which to do their washing. The posts firmly planted and marked, they walked slowly back to camp, talking over the prospects and mapping out their future work.

It was decided to move the tents to a more convenient locality, and a spot was readily found at a point above where the two gulches joined, or rather where the one gulch split into two. The transfer to this new home-spot was made the next day by Earl, Randy, and the doctor, Mr. Portney and the captain going back to uncover several other portions of the claims, to ascertain, if possible, just what their values might be.

The next week was a busy one. The camp removed and put into comfortable shape, the next work was to dam up the gulch where the pocket had been found, so that all the water might flow through Mosquito Hollow, as the doctor had facetiously dubbed the new diggings, — a name that stuck to it. This work was done by Randy and Dr. Barwaithe, while Earl joined the captain and his uncle in burning down the brush and getting rid of the tundra.

Before turning the water from Prosper Gulch into Mosquito Hollow, Foster Portney advised sinking several holes along the latter gulch, that any gold washed along by the flow would be caught. The captain put these down, and then came the long labor of cleaning the sand and dirt from the bedrock below. As it would have taken all summer to clean out the entire bottom of the gulch, only the deeper part was attacked and here a runway for the water was made, a foot to two feet wide.

The water had just been turned along Mosquito Hollow and washing begun when a party of prospectors from Forty Mile Post came along and espied the claims. They at once wished to know the particulars of the find made, and, assured that there was gold there, one of the men lost no time in putting up his stakes below them, while two others went above. Inside of a week after this the Hollow boasted of eight claims, and a little settlement sprung up at the Fork, as the miners named the spot where the Portney crowd had located.

"We'll have a town here before the summer is over," said Earl; but he was not sorry to have company, especially as the newcomers were all hail-fellows-well-met and apparently honest to the core. Among them was a young lawyer from Dakota, and he and Dr. Barwaithe soon became the warmest of friends.

The short Alaska summer was now reaching its height, and flowers and berries were growing everywhere in the wildest profusion, while during the middle of the day the sun beat down so fiercely that they were often compelled to seek the shade for hours at a time.

"My gracious, the Hollow is like a pepper box!" said Randy one day, as he came into camp with his shirt wet through with perspiration. "Not a breath of air stirring."

"And the hotter it is, the worse the flies are," added Earl. "I declare, they seem to bother me more than even the mosquitoes."

Usually it cooled off toward seven or eight o'clock, even though the sun still shone well up in the sky, but this night proved as warm as the day had been, and most of the party went to sleep outdoors, unable to stand it inside of the close tents. Outside, they had to wind their heads and necks in mosquito netting and cover up their hands, to keep from being pestered to death. It was the most uncomfortable twenty-four hours they had yet put in.

"The old Harry take Alaska!" burst out Dr.

Barwaithe, finally. One mosquito had alighted on his nose, and two others on his neck. "It's worth all the gold you can get, and more, too, to stand these impudent pests. Oh!" And making half a dozen wild slashes he finally scrambled up and ran around the tents to throw his tormentors off.

The captain was suffering from a slight attack of scurvy, brought on by eating so much salt food. The doctor had given him some medicine, but this did little good, and the captain was getting into a bad way when one of the old miners, who had just come in, came to his aid.

"Eat tomatoes, cap'n," he said. "Best thing on airth fer scurvy. Bill Watson wuz down with it wust way an' nuthin' helped him but tomatoes. He eat 'most a bushel o' 'em, an' they made a new man o' him. Eat tomatoes."

"Tomatoes may be very good," said the doctor. "They are a very strong, green vegetable, you know. You might try them."

And the captain did try them, first using up some of the cans brought along, and then buying a quart of fresh tomatoes at Dawson City, for two dollars. Sure enough, the tomatoes helped wonderfully, and about a week later the scurvy left him.

Nearly a month had now passed since the party had located at Mosquito Hollow, and in that time they had taken out three small nuggets worth probably fifty dollars apiece, and a little short of a hundred and fifty ounces of gold dust. Counting the gold dust as worth sixteen dollars an ounce, this gave them, in round figures, twenty-five hundred dollars for their labor.

"Twenty-five hundred dollars!" said Earl. "That's a good deal more than we could earn at home."

Captain Zoss gave a deep sigh and shook his head. "I ain't satisfied," he said. "I didn't come up to Alaska to work fer no five hundred a month. I'm goin' elsewhar fer luck."

"You won't stay here?" asked Randy, quickly. He had begun to like the captain very much.

"No, lad; I'm yere to make a fortune or nuthin'. I quit the hollow ter-morrow."

"Well, you have that right, captain, although I'm sorry to see you go," said Foster Portney.

"Which means thet you an' the boys stay," answered the captain, quickly. "I'm sorry ye won't go with me. I want ter try Hunker Creek."

"I think I'll stay," said Foster Portney, quietly. "I'll give the gulch a few weeks longer, for the way I look at it we're making wages and have the chance to make a strike. What do you say, boys?"

Randy was in for following the captain, but a look from Earl made him change the words on the end of his tongue. "I'll do as you think best, Uncle Foster."

"And so will I," said Earl.

Then they looked at the doctor, who was kicking the

toe of his boot against the tent pole in speculative way. It was several seconds before the medical man spoke.

"I — I think I'll go with the captain," he said finally. "Not but that I hate to part company," he added hastily. "But I came up here to make a big hit, and if I wanted to work for what we've been making here, I could get it easier by going into Dawson City and hanging out my shingle — you all know that. I hope we part the best of friends."

"We will," said Foster Portney. "We'll divide our gold as per agreement, and also the outfits."

"And I'll give you my share of this gulch free," said the captain, and the doctor said the same.

Of this, however, Foster Portney would not hear. He insisted on paying each of them a hundred dollars, and drawing up regular papers, which were signed in the presence of two of the outside miners. On the day following the doctor and the captain packed up their traps, hired four Indians to help them, and set off, first however, giving Mr. Portney and each of the boys a hearty handshake. In a few minutes they were out of sight.

"And now to work the Hollow for all it is worth," said Foster Portney, when they were left alone. "And remember, from henceforth, whatever we turn up belongs to us and to nobody else."

CHAPTER XXIV.

AN UNLOOKED-FOR ARRIVAL.

ALTHOUGH the boys missed Dr. Barwaithe and Captain Zoss greatly, there was much of satisfaction in the thought that their uncle had expressed; namely, that henceforth whatever was taken out of the three claims on Mosquito Hollow gulch would belong to them and to nobody else.

"Of course, we can't expect to do as much work as was done before," was the way Earl reasoned. "But we are just as liable as ever to make a big strike."

During the following week the weather turned off somewhat cooler, and this made work easier and more rapid. All three went at it with a will, and the six days brought in six hundred dollars in dust.

"That's a hundred and fifty apiece for us, Earl," said Randy, after figuring up. "It beats lumbering down in Maine all hollow, doesn't it?"

"I'll tell you better after we've gone through a winter up here, Randy. From all accounts the weather is something awful, and we've got to stand it, for getting away is out of the question after the first of September."

"Well, let's not anticipate trouble. I guess Uncle will see that we are as well provided for as possible," answered Randy, who could think of nothing but the gold dust brought in daily.

So far they had done all their washing with hand pans. Foster Portney had tried to obtain a cradle, or a "Long Tom," but had failed. Now he announced his intention to go over to the saw-mill at Dawson and buy the necessary boards for several sluice boxes. He left on Friday, stating he would probably not return before Monday or Tuesday.

The week had brought a number of newcomers to the vicinity, who had staked claims on other gulches within a radius of half a mile. Some of these late arrivals had come over the mountain pass, while the majority had taken the longer route up the Pacific Ocean and the Yukon. The Fork seemed to be a favorite camping ground, and there were times when as many as a score of tents were pitched there.

One of the newcomers was from Hunker Creek, and he brought news of the doctor and the captain. The pair had staked two claims some distance above Discovery and were doing fairly well, although they had by no means struck it as rich as anticipated.

It was on Saturday evening, when Randy and Earl were busy washing out some of their underwear — for they of course had to play their own washerwoman — that news was brought to them that there was a young fellow down at a camp below who had expressed a desire that Randy or Earl come to see him.

"He ain't give no name, but he's a slim-built chap an' don't look like he was cut out fer roughing it," said the messenger. "He's half sick, and he was grub-struck when me and my pard picked him up."

"A slim-built chap—" began Randy, when Earl broke in: "It's Fred Dobson, the crazy fool!"

"Fred!" cried Randy. He turned to the messenger and asked the miner to give him a better description of the boy; but this was not forthcoming, and he hurried off with the man, leaving Earl in charge of the tent.

The camp below was quarter of a mile away, over a hill thick with blackberry bushes. But something like a trail had been tramped down from the Fork, and it did not take the two long to cover the distance. They had just come over the hill in sight of several tents when Randy beheld somebody get up from a seat on a fallen log and totter toward him.

"Randy Portney!" It was Fred Dobson's voice, but so thin and hollow Randy scarcely recognized it. "Oh, how glad I am to see somebody I know!"

"Fred! How in the world did you get up here!" burst out Randy. He took the hand of the squire's son, and led the way back to the seat. "How thin and pale you look! I thought you had gone back to Basco!"

Fred heaved a deep sigh. Then he looked Randy

full in the face for a moment. His eyes were moist, and he tried in vain to keep back the tears. But it was impossible, and throwing his head on Randy's shoulder, he wept like a child.

The tears touched Randy to the heart, and he caught the thin hands and pressed them warmly. "Never mind, Fred," he said. "Now you are up here I'll do what I can for you. So let up and tell me your story."

It was several minutes before Fred could do this. "I came up by the way of the Chilkoot Pass," he said, when he felt able to speak. "I joined a party I met in Juneau, a crowd of men from Chicago, and they promised to see me through if I would do my share of work. But the work was too hard for me, and they treated me like a dog, and at Baker's Creek they kicked me out of camp and compelled me to shift for myself."

"How long ago was this?"

"A week ago. Since that time I've been knocking around from pillar to post, looking for something I could do, so as to earn at least enough to eat. I did get one job in Dawson City washing dishes in the restaurant, but even there the food the boss wanted me to eat was more than I could stand, as it was nothing but leavings."

"And when did you hear of us?"

"Yesterday. I struck a miner named Wodley and he gave me your directions. Oh, Randy, what a fool I was to come to Alaska! If only I had taken your advice and gone back to Basco!" And it was only by an effort that Fred Dobson kept himself from crying anew. He felt miserable, weak, and hungry, had had scarcely a kind word for weeks, and was on the point of giving up in despair.

"Do your parents know where you are?" asked Randy, after another pause.

"Yes, I wrote to them just before leaving Juneau — I couldn't think of going so far away without doing that."

"Well, that was at least one sensible move, Fred." Randy thought for a moment. "Our camp is about half a mile from here, over that hill. Can you walk that far?"

"Oh, yes, Randy; I can walk a good way now I've found a friend." Fred arose as quickly as he could. "Are you and your friends all together yet?"

"No; there are only my uncle, Earl, and myself now."

The two were soon on the journey over the hill. Fred was still rather shaky, and Randy gave him his arm to help him at the difficult places. When they reached camp, Earl had all the washing out and everything tidied up.

"So it is you, Fred?" he said, as he held out his hand. "I thought you back in Basco by this time."

"I only wish I was! I made the biggest mistake

of my life when I ran away, so there! and I don't care who knows it!" And Fred threw himself on a bench in front of the tent.

"If there is any of that bean soup left, you had better give Fred some," said Randy, with a knowing glance which did not escape Earl. "And I'm going to fry some of the fish I caught over in the river last night."

Half an hour later the wanderer was sitting down to as appetizing a supper as he had tasted since leaving the States. While he ate he told his story in detail, to which Randy and Earl listened with much interest. That Fred had had a hard time of it there could be no doubt; and that he had learned a lesson he would never forget was also apparent.

"If there was only some way of getting home, I'd start to-morrow," he said. "But I'm up here now, and I've got to do for myself — somehow." He looked wistfully at Earl and Randy. "Do you think I could make some kind of a deal with your uncle to keep me? I know I am not as strong and hardy as you, but I can do something, and I won't look for any pay."

"I don't know what uncle will say," said Earl. "He has gone to Dawson, and won't be back before Monday or Tuesday. I guess you can stay here till that time."

"Yes; and if he won't take you in, I'll help you

some," added Randy. "We've been more fortunate than you."

Fred was curious to know how they had made out, and Earl and Randy told him. He was amazed to think they had done so well; and his face brightened a good deal when he remembered how Randy had said he would help him.

Sunday was spent in camp. Fred, who was completely tired out, slept the greater part of the day, although at meal times, weak as he was, he insisted on washing the dishes and the pots and kettles, just to show that he was in earnest about working. This made Earl and Randy smile to themselves.

"Think of Fred washing dishes like that at home," whispered Earl to his brother. "If only the squire could see him now, I guess he'd almost forgive him for running away!"

On Monday the two brothers went to work as usual in the Hollow. Fred followed them over and was much interested in their labors. Once he tried shovelling up the sand and dirt, but Earl told him he had better take it easy and get back his strength; and then he walked back to the tent, to spend the balance of the day in mending his clothing, which was sadly in need of repairs. When the boys came back, he had supper ready for them, and never had they had a meal in camp that was better cooked.

"Cooking was the one thing I learned coming up

here," Fred explained. "There was a negro in the party who had been a chef in a Chicago hotel; and he was the one soul in the crowd that treated me half decently."

"Perhaps uncle will retain you as cook," said Randy, mischievously, and then he stopped short, for he did not wish to hurt Fred's feelings. The supper passed off pleasantly, and Fred announced that he felt a hundred times better than the day previous.

It was around ten o'clock, and the sun had just set over the mountains to the westward, leaving the Hollow in an uncertain, pale-blue light, which would last until sunrise at four, when a messenger on muleback dashed along the trail from Gold Bottom. "Thar's a lynchin' goin' on down to Smedley's!" he yelled, as he sped by. "They've caught a sneak thief by the name o' Guardley, an' they're goin' ter make him do er dance on nuthin'. Better be gittin' down thar, if ye want ter see justice done!"

CHAPTER XXV.

MORE WORK IN THE GULCHES.

"THEY are going to lynch a fellow named Guardley!" ejaculated Earl. "I wonder if it can be Jasper Guardley."

"It must be; it's not likely there is another Guardley up here — the name isn't as common as all that, returned Randy. "Shall we go?"

Earl hesitated. There was something appalling in a lynching, to his mind. Yet he was curious to know more of the crime for which the prisoner was about to suffer.

"Yes, we might as well — if Fred will watch the camp," he answered.

"I'll watch it as well as I can," answered Fred. The work he had been doing had tired him more than he would admit, and he was glad enough to take it easy. He knew Guardley, but took small interest in the man his father had sent up more than once for petty crimes.

In less than five minutes Earl and Randy were off, stalking over the hills and along Gold Bottom Creek as rapidly as their tired limbs would carry them. Smedley's, a settlement of twoscore of tents and one board cabin where a few odds and ends could be bought, was nearly two miles distance, yet they arrived there in less than half an hour — fast time when the state of the trails they had travelled was taken into consideration.

They found that the prisoner had been bound, hands and feet, and placed in the storeroom of the board cabin, a little shed in the rear, scarcely eight feet by twelve and hardly high enough for a man to stand in. Two rough-looking miners were on guard, one with a gun, and the other with an old-fashioned horse-pistol over a foot long.

"What do you want?" demanded one of the miners of Earl, as the latter pushed his way forward through the fast-gathering crowd. "This ain't no place fer a young rooster like you."

"I would like to see the prisoner, please," answered Earl. "I think I know him."

"You ain't the feller's pard, are ye?" demanded the second guard, suspiciously.

"No. I am from Maine, and I knew a Guardley up there who came to these diggings. I wanted to find out if it was the same man."

"Say, is that Earl Portney?" came from within, and both Earl and Randy recognized Jasper Guardley's voice. "If it is, I'd like to talk to him."

"Yes, Guardley," answered Earl. "What's the trouble?"

"I WOULD LIKE TO SEE THE PRISONER, PLEASE." — *Page 196.*

"Can't you come in and talk to me?"

"I'll come in if the guards will allow it," and Earl looked at the men.

"Go on in; but leave yer gun with me, if yer got one," was the reply, from the man who had first addressed Earl.

"I haven't any pistol," said the youth, and passed into the shed. Randy was about to follow, but the guard stopped him. "One's enough, my lad; you wait outside." And Randy fell back into the crowd, which kept increasing every minute.

From those around him, Randy learned that Guardley was being held for the theft of eighty ounces of gold dust, which had been buried by a miner, named Cozzins, under the flooring of his tent. Cozzins had missed his gold that morning, and three other miners had testified to seeing Guardley sneaking around the place, in company with another man, presumably Tom Roland. Roland and the gold were both gone, and Guardley had been "collared" just as he was about to leave for Dawson City. The miners around Smedley's had held a meeting, and it was likely that Guardley's crime would cost him his life.

"For you see we ain't got no jails here," explained one miner. "An' to leave sech a measly critter run would be puttin' a premium on crime."

When Earl came out of the shed his face was very pale, and he was on the point of passing the guards without a word, when they stopped him. "Well, wot did ye make out?" demanded one, laconically.

"He says he didn't take the gold — that the robbery was planned and executed by his partner. It is awful to think of taking his life."

"It's his own fault, lad — he should have thunk o' those things afore he consented to help on the job."

"When will they — they — "

"Perform the ceremony? I reckon some time between now an' sunrise, onless the crowd changes its mind. They're goin' to talk it over agin ez soon as Cozzins comes back. He's huntin' fer thet other rascal."

After this Earl joined Randy, who was anxious to hear what Guardley had had to say. The two walked some distance away.

"I believe Tom Roland stole the gold," began Earl, "but Guardley was willing he should, and he remained on guard around the tent while Roland dug it up, so he's just as guilty."

"But to take his life —" shuddered Randy.

"I hope they change their minds about that. And, by the way, we were right about that money in Boston. Roland got that, and he had that lost letter, too. Guardley admitted it, although he didn't give me any particulars. He is trying to lay the blame of everything on Roland."

A shout interrupted the conversation at this point. Cozzins had come back after an exciting but fruitless chase. At his appearance the scene took on a new activity, and the would-be lynching party moved to the front of the so-called store, where half a dozen flaring torches and two smoking kerosene lamps lit up the weird scene. Here Cozzins told his story, and then Guardley was brought out, trembling in every limb. He begged over and over again to be let go, and his earnestness had its effect even on the man who had been robbed. A talk lasting a quarter of an hour followed, and then Guardley was given his choice of two sentences,— the one being that already pronounced, and the other being a whip-lashing on his bare back, and a drumming out of the camp, with the warning that if he ever showed up there again, he was to be shot on sight. With a long sigh of relief he chose the latter punishment, and was ordered to strip, while Cozzins prepared for his part in the affair, by hunting up the hardest and strongest rawhide dog-whip to be found.

"I don't want to see the whipping," whispered Randy; "let us go home. Poor Guardley! I guess Cozzins will make him suffer as he has never suffered before!"

"I hope it teaches him a lesson to turn over a new leaf," answered Earl. "But I'm afraid there isn't any reform to Guardley. He hasn't even enough manliness to shoulder his share of the blame, but tries to put it all off on Roland. Come on." And they turned away without another word. Before they were out of hearing distance of the camp, a shriek rent the air, telling that Guardley's punishment had already begun.

The boys had expected their uncle to come back by Tuesday as told; but in the afternoon one of the miners, working down Mosquito Hollow, brought word from Dawson City that Mr. Portney could not get his lumber for two or three days, and might be absent the remainder of the week in consequence. So there was nothing to do but to keep on working at the claims with the hand pans, and this Randy and Earl did, Fred helping them as far as he was able. The boy who had been so ill-treated and half starved was growing stronger rapidly, and he showed a willingness to do even the most disagreeable things which was as astonishing as it was gratifying.

Friday found the trio working up along a little split in the rocks on the right bank of the gulch. The split was not over two feet wide by twelve feet long, and it was filled with gravel and muck, with here and there the nest of a field mouse among the tundra. Earl had suggested clearing out the split, and he had gone in first to loosen the gravel with his pick. About three loads of soil had been removed and carted down to the gulch stream, and now Earl found the balance of the split blocked by a huge rock.

"Doesn't seem to amount to much," he said, throwing down his tools to mop the perspiration from his brow.

"Let me go in there," suggested Fred, and caught up the pick. Swinging the tool over his shoulder, he brought it down with all force at a spot where the rock showed a slight crack.

"Look out, or you'll break that pick!" called out Randy, when the front half of the rock fell away, and Fred had to jump up to avoid having his feet crushed. As he made the leap, his eyes caught sight of a surface of yellow half hidden by muck and moss. He struck at it with the pick, and out came a nugget nearly as big as his fist. He grabbed it up in a transport of delight.

"Look! look! A nugget! Oh, what a big fellow! How much do you think it's worth?" he cried; and rubbed the muck off with his coat sleeve. "It looks as if it was solid!"

"It is almost solid," said Earl, weighing the find in his hand. "It's worth two or three hundred dollars at least." And then he added, by way of a caution, "You'll have to remember, Fred, that this is my uncle's claim."

"Oh, I know that. But it ought to be worth something for finding it," said Fred, wistfully.

"Certainly, we'll make it right."

"Of course we will," added Randy. "Let us see if there are any more nuggets in there. This may be a pocket, like the one I found on Prosper Gulch." He went forward, but Earl was ahead of him, and was using the pick with all the speed and skill at his command. As the remainder of the rock came away, a mass of sand, gravel, and dirt followed.

"Here are four small nuggets," said Randy, picking them up. "Fifty-dollar finds, every one of them."

Earl said nothing, although he heard the talk. He had espied a gleam of dull yellow wedged in between the side of the split and a second rock. He tried to force the second rock out, and as it moved forward the gleam of yellow became larger and larger, until his hand could not have covered it. He worked on frantically, hardly daring to breathe. At last the rock fell and the face of the nugget lay revealed, shaped very much like the sole and heel of a large man's shoe.

"What have you got?" asked Randy and Fred simultaneously, seeing something was up; but Earl kept right on, picking away below the find, and to both sides. It seemed to him the thing would never come out, and as he realized how large the nugget was, his hands trembled so he could scarcely hold the pick. "I've struck a fortune!" he muttered, at last, in a strangely hoarse voice. "See if anybody is looking, Randy." And then the nugget came loose, and he clutched it in both hands and held it up, — a dull, dirty, yellowish lump, worth at least three thousand dollars!

CHAPTER XXVI.

SLUICE BOXES AND PREPARATIONS FOR WINTER.

A NUGGET worth three thousand dollars was, by far, the largest find yet made in that district, and the three young miners could scarcely believe it true, as they surveyed the lump in Earl's hands.

"Do you suppose it's pure gold?" asked Randy, as he took it from his brother. "It's heavy enough."

"I think it's almost pure," said Earl. "We've struck it rich this time. Be sure and keep your mouth shut, both of you, or we'll have all of Gold Bottom up here," he added. "We've got at least four thousand dollars' worth of stuff out of there, so far, and goodness only knows how much more there is."

"Here come a couple of miners now," whispered Fred, happening to glance down the gulch. He dropped some of the smaller nuggets into his pockets, while Randy took care of the rest. Earl let the large lump fall into the dirt and covered it up with tundra muck.

"Well, pards, how air ye makin' it?" asked one of the miners, as he halted on the edge of the gulch.

"Oh, we're doing fairly well," answered Earl, as coolly as he could, although still highly excited. "Where are you bound?"

"Thought we'd try it over to Hunker Creek. Some good reports from there this week."

"So I've heard," said Randy. "I wonder if it would pay us to go over."

"It might — everybody has an equal chance, ye know," said the second miner. "Say, do ye calkerlate to git anything outer thet split?" he went on, with a look of disdain on his face.

"I thought I would see what was in it," said Earl. "If a fellow don't try, he'll never find anything."

"Ye won't git nuthin' out o' thar; the split don't lay right. Better go up to the top end o' your claim; ye'll stand more chance thar." And after a few words more the two miners moved off, and the boys breathed easier.

"That shows what he knows about it," said Earl, when he dared to broach the subject. "Wouldn't he open his eyes if he knew the truth?"

"And wouldn't he be in for squeezing a claim right on top of us?" added Randy. "No; we had best keep this find to ourselves, at least until we've found just what is in the split and how far away from the gulch it runs."

"Throw all the nuggets into the hole over yonder," said Earl, "and cover them up. We'll take them to the tent to-night, and bury them in some safe place. I'm going ahead." And he began to pick away as though his life depended upon it, while Randy and Fred went over the sand, gravel, and dirt with their shovels and hands, to pick out some small nuggets, which they found to the number of forty-three, some not larger than a grain of rice, and others the size of coffee beans.

"Here is another lump," said Earl, presently, and brought out a thin sheet of gold, mixed with stone. "I shouldn't wonder if there is a layer of quartz rock somewhere along here, although I don't see anything of it yet. I guess this lump will produce thirty or forty dollars' worth of gold more. Pretty good for five minutes' work." And he went at it again with renewed vigor, scattering the sand and gravel behind him, like a mother hen looking for worms.

An hour later the split was cleaned out so far as it could be accomplished with the tools at hand. There remained a small crack still, running downward three feet, as Earl ascertained by testing it with a berry-bush switch. What there might be at the bottom of the crack there was no telling, although it must contain some gold, if only in dust. Three additional nuggets had been unearthed, one as large as a pint measure and finer in appearance than any of the rest. Making sure they were not observed, the first nuggets were again brought forth, and each took a portion of them to carry home. The largest was tied up in Earl's coat, which he slung carelessly over his shoulder as he trudged along.

"Worth five to six thousand dollars if they are worth a cent," said Earl, as he surveyed the lot in the privacy of their tent. "And we haven't begun to wash up yet nor tested that little crack. This is the best luck yet."

Some of their findings had already been put down in a hole under the bedding in the tent. The hole was now opened and the new findings added, Earl first making a list of the nuggets, to give to his uncle. The ground was pounded down hard after this, so that if anybody wanted to dig the treasure up, he would find it a day's labor. Nearly all the miners buried their large finds, it being the only protection to be had.

On Saturday Mr. Portney came back, bringing with him three Indians loaded down with lumber and hardware. He was much surprised to see Fred, and was on the point of giving the lad a good talking to when Randy called him aside and explained the situation. Earl, also, put in a good word for Fred; and then, when the Indians were paid off and discharged, the subject was dropped, by both boys telling of the wonderful find which had been made. Of course Foster Portney was greatly interested, and he smiled when Randy particularly mentioned how Fred had brought out the first nugget and caused Earl to investigate further.

"You certainly deserve credit for that, Dobson," he said. "You shall have your full share of whatever the nugget proves to be worth. As for that little split, the only thing we can do is to blow it open with dynamite, and, luckily, I brought a can of the stuff from Dawson for just such an emergency."

Foster Portney had heard about Guardley, and had also heard that some Canadian mounted police, who had arrived at Dawson City, were on Tom Roland's trail. Guardley had turned up at Forty Mile Post whipped half to death, and it was doubtful whether he would get over his punishment.

On Sunday the question of whether Fred Dobson should remain as one of the party or not was fully discussed. The lad offered to work for nothing if only given his board and such clothing as he needed, and Randy and Earl said Fred could certainly cook as well as any of them and was getting more used to using a pick and a shovel every day. Seeing that his nephews wanted the runaway to be taken in, Mr. Portney at last said he would "let it go at that."

"I'll feed you and clothe you," he added, "and if we come out all right next spring I'll pay your passage back to Basco and give you a little extra in the bargain. But you've got to hustle the same as the rest of us; that is, as far as your strength and health will permit." And Fred said he understood and was thankful for the chance, and would do his level best.

And he did do his level best from that hour forth. His experience had been a bitter one, but at the same time it had been the best in the world for him, — exactly what he needed.

The days which followed were busy ones. With the lumber brought in, Foster Portney and the boys constructed three sluice boxes, which, after completion, were set up at convenient points in the gulch, where the water might easily be turned on and off in them. Each box was fifteen feet long and a foot square, open at each end and at the top, the latter having a few braces across to keep the sides stiff. At the bottom of the box small cleats about an inch high were placed at intervals of fifteen inches apart, the last cleat, at the lower end of the box, being a trifle higher than the rest.

A sluice box done, it was carried to the spot selected for it and planted firmly, with its lower end in the stream and its upper end elevated from one to two feet. Then the upper end of the stream was run into it by means of a water trough. The box was now ready for use. By shovelling dirt in at the upper end and allowing the water to run through, the dirt was gradually washed down and out at the lower end, leaving the heavy gold to settle to the bottom and pile up along the upper sides of the cleats previously mentioned. At night the water was turned aside and the day's accumulation of gold was scraped away from the cleats.

"We can do a good deal more with the boxes than we can with the pans," said Foster Portney. "And what washing we want to do must be done before cold weather sets in and the gulch freezes up."

It must not be supposed that the slit in the rocks had been forgotten. To the contrary, all hands had often spoken of it, and as soon as the sluice boxes were finished every one in the claim turned to the place. Two sticks of dynamite were placed in the slit and set off, and the rock blown into a thousand fragments.

The blast revealed an opening beneath the slit which was a yard wide and twice as deep. This opening was filled with loose sand and dirt, and at the bottom of all was a thick layer of gold dust, slightly mixed with silver. They scraped the dust up with great care, and found that it would very nearly fill a quart measure. They hunted eagerly for nuggets, but no more could be found, and the quartz rock Earl had hoped for failed to appear.

"Never mind; we can't expect too much luck," said Mr. Portney. "A heap of dust like this is find enough for one day. Let us scrape the hole thoroughly and cart the dirt down to the nearest sluice box." This was done and they examined the vicinity carefully for another slit, but none appeared. This pocket, like that on Prosper Gulch, was now exhausted, and with a sigh Randy and Earl turned away to the regular work of washing for dust. Each had one of the boxes allotted

P

to him, while Foster Portney took the third. Fred occupied his time between the three and in cooking the meals; and thus the balance of the summer slipped by until the day came when Mr. Portney announced that they must begin building a cabin and prepare for the long Alaskan winter which would speedily close in around them.

CHAPTER XXVII.

THE END OF THE SUMMER SEASON.

MR. PORTNEY and the boys had long since decided where the cabin should be built, up against the side of a cliff, ten feet in height, which overlooked the head of the gulch. All the miners in the locality had agreed that this would be the best spot, and six cabins were to be placed there, for hospitality's sake if for no other reason. Mr. Portney had already ordered the dressed lumber needed from the saw-mill; but as this was costly stuff, and expensive to transport, Earl and Randy had declared their intention to go into the timber back of the cliff and get out whatever of rough wood could be made to do.

"We're not going in for style," declared Earl. "You can get the window frames and glass, and the door and the finishing boards, and we'll get out the rest, won't we, Randy?" And his brother agreed with him.

A week later found the party building in earnest. Over a hundred dollars' worth of lumber had been purchased, and it had cost as much again to bring it over. In the meantime Earl and Randy, aided by Fred, had brought out from the woods four sticks of timber for the corner posts of the cabin and had whip-sawed two-score of rough boards. With this material they went to work, and four pairs of willing hands soon caused the building to take definite shape. Seeing them at work, the other miners also got at it, and soon there was sawing and hammering all day long beneath the cliff.

Of necessity the cabin was a simple affair. It was set partly on the flat rock and partly on the hard ground, and was twenty feet wide by twelve feet deep, the back resting almost against the cliff. In the front was a door and a window, and there was another window at the end nearest to the door. Inside, a spare blanket divided the space into two compartments, the first, the one having the door, being the general living-room, and the second being the sleeping-room. In the living-room was placed a cooking-stove, a rude table, and four home-made chairs, while the sleeping-room was provided with four bunks, ranged along the rear and end walls. Later on a closet was built for the cooking-utensils, but for the present these were piled up in a corner.

Foster Portney was very particular that all the cracks in the side walls of the cabin should be filled in with mud, and the top, which was nearly on a level with the cliff, was also made water and wind tight, excepting where a circular hole was left for the upper section of a stovepipe.

As soon as the cabin was in habitable shape, an

account of all the provisions on hand was taken. It was found that the canned vegetables had run low and that they also needed more flour. A list of necessities was made out, and Earl and his uncle started away to Dawson City to purchase them, knowing that prices were advancing every day and that the goods on hand at the store were liable to give out long before the demand for them should cease.

Fred had asked to go out into the woods to see what he could shoot, he being a fairly good shot and thoroughly familiar with the use of a gun. It was thought best not to let him go alone, and he and Randy went together, leaving the cabin in care of the miners who were building close at hand.

The hunt in the woods was hardly a success. After tramping around for two hours they brought down several birds of a species unknown to them and one small deer, smaller than any Randy had ever seen in Maine. Otherwise the woods were bare of game, and by the middle of the afternoon they gave it up.

"When Earl comes back I'll ask my uncle to let the three of us go over to the river," said Randy. "I've heard there are good chances there for wild goose, snipe, and plover."

"Yes, and we might put in a day fishing. Even salt and smoked fish wouldn't go bad during the winter," added Fred. He was growing hardy and strong and took a deep interest in all that was going on.

It was two days before Mr. Portney and Earl returned, bringing with them all they and two Indians could carry. The provisions included an extra hundred pounds of flour, for which they had paid fifty dollars, some canned peas and tomatoes, fifteen pounds of dried apples and California apricots, and some coffee, sugar, salt, and smoked bacon. In an extra package Earl also carried a beefsteak weighing two pounds and for which he had paid five dollars.

"It's Randy's birthday to-morrow," he said, "and we're going to celebrate in a style I know you'll all admire." And every one laughed and agreed with him, for they had not had any fresh beef since leaving the steamboat at Dyea.

Foster Portney was quite willing that the three boys should take a trip over to the Yukon to see what could be found in the way of fish and game, and it was arranged that they should be gone three days. The start was made on Monday morning.

They travelled altogether by compass through the woods, managing on the way to knock over enough birds to serve them for their meals. On the morning of the second day they struck the Yukon about midway between Dawson City and Ogilvie. As they came in sight of the broad stream Earl halted the crowd and pointed straight ahead.

"Look at the snipe!" he said. "Now is our chance. Let us all fire together!"

Randy and Fred had borrowed shot-guns from their neighbors, and at the signal three reports rang out, and eight of the birds came down. A second shot from Randy, whose gun had a double barrel, brought down three more; and from that hour on the sport began, lasting until well into the evening, when they had twenty snipe, six plover, and eight wild geese to their credit.

As late as it was, Earl determined to try his hand at fishing, and soon had his line out. There were a few minutes of waiting, then the bait was taken like a flash, and there followed a lively struggle between the youth and a salmon which weighed over fifteen pounds. Several times Earl thought he had lost his catch, but each time he recovered, and finally the salmon came in close enough to be swung on shore. Even then he flopped around so lively that Fred had to quiet him by a blow from the stock of his gun.

Earl's success had fired the others, and soon they were fishing in the pale-blue twilight of the night. They kept it up until after twelve o'clock, when they turned in with a catch of three salmon, several whitefish, and a burbot, which Randy at first took for a codfish. They slept soundly, and early in the morning tried the sport again, starting for home at about noon, and arriving there with their burdens some time after midnight, worn out but happy.

It was found that Foster Portney had not been idle

during their absence. From time to time, as the canned eatables were disposed of, they had saved the tins, and now he had cleaned them out and filled some with such berries as still remained on the bushes about the gulch. To seal the cans up he had brought from Dawson City a stick of lead, and for an iron had used the end of a broken pick.

"That will give us some fresh berries," he said. "And along with canned salmon, and salted and smoked whitefish, burbot, and wild goose, I reckon we'll get along fairly well, unless the winter proves an extra long one."

As much as they felt the necessity of preparing for winter, Randy and Earl hated to lose the time when there was the chance to make so much money at the sluice boxes. So as soon as they were able, they got down to the gulch again, and never did two lads work harder. They were accompanied by Fred, and a day later their uncle also joined them.

The dirt from the pocket had been cleaned up, and it had yielded over twenty ounces of gold. They were now working on the regular sand and gravel scraped from the bedrock of the gulch, and though this did not pay so well, yet it brought in enough to make them all satisfied. There was a good deal of excitement, too, when it came to cleaning out the sluice boxes, for almost every day one or another found a nugget, sometimes small, and then again as large as a walnut.

"How much do you think we are averaging?" asked Randy, one day, and his uncle replied that he could not figure very closely, but he would put it down as over a hundred dollars per day. This meant twenty-five dollars a day as the boy's share, and he felt more content than ever to slave along in the gulch.

For it was slaving along, this constantly picking and digging and carting the dirt, sand, and gravel to the sluice boxes and throwing it in. Every night Randy's back ached, and sometimes he would come in with feet that were sopping wet, and covered up to his waist with mud and muck. And then he took a touch of the chills and fever, and was down on his back for a week with only Fred to wait on him. The chills and fever went the rounds, and Foster Portney and Earl were stricken at the same time. Fred was the last to catch it; and by the time he had recovered, winter was at hand.

The first indication was a rawness in the air, which made them shiver when they turned out in the morning. Then the bushes and the trees quickly lost their leaves, and three days later ice formed in the marshes back of the gulch. The sun came up as usual, but it seemed to have lost its warmth, and all were glad enough to keep on their coats even when working.

"Two more weeks will fetch it," observed Foster Portney. "We had better wash out as much dirt as possible before the water stops running."

Ten days later the thermometer went down with a rush, dropping from fifty-six to but twenty above zero. Going down to the gulch, they found the stream covered with ice, which was half an inch thick. By the next day there was no water to be found, only ice, and even the piles of sand, gravel, and dirt were frozen stiff. A heavy dulness, which oppressed them greatly, hung in the air. Winter had come, and gold washing for that season was a thing of the past.

CHAPTER XXVIII.

SNOWED IN.

ALTHOUGH everything in the gulch was frozen up, it must not be supposed that mining there came to an end. While it was true no more washing could be done that season, there was dirt, gravel, and sand to be heaped in convenient spots, ready for the first run of water in the spring.

At one end of the claims there was a bank which had been examined by Foster Portney and found to contain very rich pay dirt, and this bank was now attacked by all hands and the dirt brought out to the nearest sluice box. To thaw the ground a fire was built up against the bank every night and allowed to burn until morning. Even in extremely cold weather this thawed the bank to a depth of several feet, and when they had scooped out a hole which resembled a baker's oven the thawing-out process was still more effectual.

But it was hard and bitter work at the best, and as the cold increased, Fred found he could not stand it, and had to remain in the cabin the greater part of the time, coming out only during the middle of the day.

"This cold gets into the marrow of a fellow's bones," he said to Randy. "I don't see how you can put up with it."

"Earl and I were used to pretty tough weather up in the Maine woods, as you know," replied Randy. "I guess an out-and-out city chap would freeze stiff before he had been here a week. The thermometer was down to six below zero this morning."

The cold had cut off their water supply, and every drop for drinking or cooking had to be obtained by melting ice on the stove. To keep them in fuel, all hands spent four days up in the woods cutting timber, which was allowed to dry out for two weeks, and was then hauled over to the edge of the cliff and tumbled down to a spot between their cabin and that of their nearest neighbor, two hundred feet away.

By Foster Portney's advice another trip was made by him and Earl to the Yukon River in search of fish for winter use, for fish could now be kept by simply being frozen in a chunk of ice and laid away. The two found the ice on the Yukon over two feet thick, and had to cut fishing-holes with an axe they had brought along for that purpose. They spent a day on the river, fishing and spearing, and were rewarded with a catch of over fifty pounds. Earl had brought the shot-gun, and to the fish were added a dozen small sea-fowl, which were caught on the wing while flying southward.

"We had better be getting back," observed Foster

Portney, early on the following morning. "Unless I am greatly mistaken we shall have a heavy fall of snow by to-night."

As they did not wish to be caught in a storm, they started on the return to the gulch as rapidly as their loads would permit. They were still in the woods when the first flakes began to fall. With the coming of the snow the wind began to rise, shaking the bare limbs above them savagely and causing a lively tumble of dead branches on every side. Not to become storm-bound, they increased their pace, reaching the lower end of the gulch by six o'clock in the evening. They could hardly see before them, so thickly did the flakes come down, and both considered themselves fortunate in having struck familiar ground. By the time the cabin was reached the snow was six inches deep.

"We thought you'd be snowed under!" cried Randy, as he opened the door to let them in. He had been watching anxiously since the snow began to fall. "It's going to be an awful night."

He was right; it was an awful night — more so than any of them had anticipated. After a hot supper they retired to their bunks to sleep, only to be aroused about midnight by the roar of the wind as it tore through the woods and along the gulch with the force of a hurricane. The snow was coming down "in chunks," as Randy put it, and mingled with it were tree branches, small brush, and dried tundra. In one corner of the cabin the wind had found a crack about six inches long and less than a sixteenth of an inch wide, and through this crack the snow had sifted over the entire floor.

"Jerusalem! the roof is coming down!" cried Earl, when they had been up a few minutes, and while his uncle was stuffing a piece of cloth in the crack mentioned. There was a great noise overhead as the hurricane tore away the top joint of the stovepipe. Through the opening poured a lot of snow, which, falling on the hot stove, sent up a cloud of steam. To stop the snow from coming in, Foster Portney climbed up on the top of the table and nailed a bit of a board over the hole.

"We can't have that stovepipe up there, that's certain," he said. "We'll have to stick it out of the side window. It won't look very elegant, but I reckon we're not keeping house on looks up here." And by their united efforts the stove was swung around in front of the little window, and the upper end of what was left of the pipe was twisted around and pointed outside, after one of the small window panes had been taken out. Around the pipe Mr. Portney fitted a square sheet of tin, obtained from an empty tomato can. Then the floor was cleared of snow and the fire started up afresh.

The hurricane, or blizzard, lasted until six o'clock in the morning, and during that time nobody thought of going to sleep again. The cabin shook and rocked, and had it not been for the shelter of the cliff would have gone to pieces. The snow kept piling higher and higher until it threatened to cut off the smokepipe again.

"Perhaps we'll have to swing the stove around to the front," said Foster Portney. "We can let the pipe out near the roof, and build a little hood over it, so that the snow from the cliff can blow right over into the gulch." And later on this was done.

"This will stop work in the gulch," said Randy. "It's too bad! What on earth are we going to do with ourselves from now until next spring?"

"We'll try to keep alive and well, Randy," returned Mr. Portney, seriously. "Remember, from now on comes the tug-of-war, as the old saying goes."

But work was not over, as Randy had surmised. To be sure, when the storm ceased at noon it was found the snow was nearly three feet deep on the level. But a day's labor sufficed to beat down a path to the bank in the gulch, and once again the fires were started and the work of getting the dirt to the sluice boxes resumed. The clearing of the storm had left it stinging cold, and all were glad enough to hustle lively in order to keep warm. They worked with their overcoats on and with their feet encased in several pairs of woollen socks, and even then spent much time around the fire, "thawing out," to use Randy's words.

The work in the bank, however, paid them well. Four days after the fall of snow, Foster Portney struck several rocks to one side of the rise and located another pocket of nuggets. They were all small fellows, the largest about the size of a hickory nut, but the nuggets numbered nearly half a hundred and caused a good deal of excitement.

"It's another fifteen hundred or two thousand dollars to our credit," said Mr. Portney. "And not only that, but this dirt is as rich as that taken from the pocket over yonder. We haven't struck a million, but we are doing remarkably well."

"I wonder how Captain Zoss and Dr. Barwaithe are making out," said Earl. They had not heard from their former partners for nearly a month, when a miner had brought word to the effect that they had just located a claim on a gulch heading into Hunker Creek, the third strike since leaving Mosquito Hollow.

"I imagine they are not doing any better than we are," replied his uncle. "If they were, we should have heard of it. It may pay to strike around, more or less, but I believe in giving a claim a fair trial before abandoning it."

Less than a week later it began to snow again. The sky was heavy, and even at midday it did not brighten up. They had gone down to the gulch directly after breakfast, but now returned to the cabin, to fix up the stovepipe as previously mentioned, and to cut enough small wood to last for several weeks. All were hard at work when they saw two white men and two Indians approaching, the latter driving before them two dog teams attached to a pair of Alaskan sledges, piled high with miners' outfits. The two men were Dr. Barwaithe and Captain Zoss.

"It's a sight good fer sore eyes to see ye ag'in!" exclaimed the captain, as he shook hands with Mr. Portney and the boys. "I couldn't keep away no longer. How are ye all?"

"We are very well," said Foster Portney. "How have you been doing?"

"Only fairly well," answered the doctor. "To tell the truth, I don't think it paid to strike out. We have a little dust, but no more, I imagine, than we should have had had we remained with you."

The pair had come over to see if they could not arrange to remain at the cabin through the winter, fearing that they would find it very lonesome if they went off by themselves. They had brought along all their things, including a stock of provisions, and were willing to pay whatever was fair in addition. As their company would no doubt prove very acceptable during the long, cheerless days to come, they were taken in without question.

"We can put up two more bunks somewhere," said Foster Portney. "And though we may be rather crowded, I reckon we'll manage it." He had taken a great fancy to the doctor, and was pleased to think he would not have to depend altogether on the boys for companionship. As for the boys, Randy declared that the presence of the jovial captain would make every day seem several hours shorter. Fred, whose story had been told in secret, also took to the newcomers, and all together they formed a happy family.

But the height of the winter was now on them, and it was destined to keep its grip for many long weeks and months to come. The storm that had started on the day the doctor and the captain arrived kept up with more or less vigor for a week, and by that time they found themselves snowed in completely. The thermometer kept going down steadily, registering as low as fifteen degrees below zero, and on more than one occasion the pail of water standing up against the side of the stove was frozen solid. To keep thoroughly warm was impossible, even though they wrapped themselves in all the clothing and blankets their outfits afforded.

CHAPTER XXIX.

WAITING AND WATCHING FOR SPRING.

"Perhaps it isn't cold! I never felt so frozen up in my life!"

It was Randy who uttered the words, as he danced around the floor of the living-room, almost on top of the stove. The fire had burned low during the night, and he had just shoved in some fresh wood and opened the draughts. Going to the little window of the sleeping-apartment, he looked through the single pane of glass at the thermometer, which hung on the casement outside. The mercury registered twenty-two degrees below zero.

"Twenty-two degrees below, and this is Christmas morning!" he went on, with another shiver. "The best thing Santa Claus can bring us is warmer weather."

"Merry Christmas!" cried Fred, tumbling out of his bunk, and his cry awoke the others, and the greeting went the whole round. The fire was now blazing with a vigor which threatened to crack the stove, yet as they talked they could see each other's breath. Every one was stamping around to get his blood in circulation.

"I'll give ye some hot coffee and Christmas flapjacks!" said the captain; and soon a smell which was most appetizing was floating through the air, and they sat down at the table, which had been placed as close to the fire as possible. Indeed, "hugging the stove" was a common trick all day long, and Fred often grumbled because he could not take the stove to bed with him. The boys were waking up to the fact that an Alaskan winter was "two winters in one," as Earl said, when compared with those experienced at home.

It had been snowing again; indeed, it snowed about half the time now, and even in the middle of the day it was so dark they could scarcely see, excepting right in front of the windows. Some time previous several Indians had appeared with fish oil and some dried fat fish to sell, and they had purchased a quantity of both for lighting purposes. The oil was used in a lamp made of a round tin having a home-made wick hanging over the side. The fat fish, dried very hard, were slit in strips and set up, to be lighted and burnt as tallow candles. Many of the Indians and the Esquimaux have no lights but these dried-fish candles. The smell from them is far from pleasant, but they are certainly better than nothing.

As it was a holiday, the boys felt they must do something. But what to do was the question, until Fred suggested they try their hand at making some candy. They were allowed just a pound of sugar by the men, and worked themselves half sick over the wood fire until noon, when the candy was declared done. It was a sort of taffy; and although it would not have added to the reputation of a skilled confectioner, all hands partook of their share of it, and declared it excellent.

Just before being snowed in Mr. Portney had become the possessor of two newspapers and a magazine, and much of the time was spent by one or another over these. The magazine was rather a heavy one, yet the boys read it through from cover to cover, including all the advertisements. It contained among other stories one which was continued, and to pass away the time they tried to invent a conclusion. This self-imposed task amused the doctor also, and he took a hand and finished the tale in a manner which took three evenings to tell.

And so New Year's Day came and went, and still they found themselves housed up with the thermometer continually at fifteen to twenty degrees below. Once it went down to twenty-six below, and everything fairly cracked with the cold. To keep from being frozen, one and another stood guard during the night, that the fire might not go down. During that time they received but scant news from their neighbors, although the cabins along the under side of the cliff were less than seventy yards apart. Nobody cared to venture out, and even opening the door was something to be considered, although the doctor insisted on having a little fresh air.

"Providence help the poor chaps who are not well provided for this winter," said Mr. Portney, one day. "I shouldn't wonder if some of them are found dead in the spring."

"To be sure," answered the captain. "I looked ter somethin' putty bad myself, but I didn't expect nuthin' like this. Why, we might jest as well be a-sittin' on the top o' the North Pole. Hain't been a blessed streak o' sunshine fer eight days, an' every time it snows the stuff piles up a foot or so more! It must be nigh on to thirty feet deep in yonder gulch."

"We'll have to economize with our store before long," put in the doctor. "Flour is running pretty low. Captain, you'll have to give us less flap-jacks — they're too toothsome."

"Yes, we'll have to come down to plain bread," said Foster Portney. "And maybe eat it stale too," he added.

Economizing began that day, after Mr. Portney had taken an account of the provisions still left to them. Whatever they had must be made to do for three months yet, and three months meant ninety days, a goodly number for which to provide.

Slowly the days wore on, every one so much like the others that it seemed impossible to tell them apart. Sunday was the one day they observed through it all. On the morning of that the doctor invariably read a chapter out of the Bible he carried, and one or another of the rest offered prayer. "It's right an' proper," said the captain, speaking of this. "We don't want ter live like no heathens, even if we are cast away in an ocean o' snow!"

February proved the worst month of all. It snowed nearly the whole time, and it was so dark that they kept the lights lit as long as they dared to consume the fish oil and the dried fish. During that time they saw or heard nothing of their neighbors, who might have died of starvation without their being any the wiser. The snow against the door was five feet high and water was obtained by shovelling this into the pot instead of ice and melting it.

"Well, it's a dog's life and that's the truth," said Earl one day, in the middle of March. "It's worth all the gold we've found — that's my opinion." It was the first time Earl had grumbled since winter set in, but as he had not had what he called a square meal for a month he can well be pardoned for the speech.

"If I thought I could get there and back, I would try for some extra provisions from Dawson," said Foster Portney; but none of the others would hear of his attempting such a trip, feeling certain he would lose his way and perish.

"We'll make out with what we have," said the doctor. "Divide the rations so they'll hold out until the middle of April. I fancy by that time this winter siege will about end." His advice was followed out, and they waited with all the patience possible for the coming of spring.

The fish and game had long since come to an end, and they were now living on plain bread, beans, and bacon or pork, and half a can of fresh vegetables per day, with an occasional taste of stewed dried apples or apricots as a side dish. They were all tired of the beans, especially Fred and the doctor, who had been used to good living all their lives.

"They're too much for me," said Fred, one day, as he pushed his small plateful back. "I'd rather eat a crust of bread and drink snow water." And the beans remained untouched for two days, when he was forced, out of sheer hunger, to go at them again.

They had also reached the last half pound of coffee, and by a general vote this was reserved for dinner each Sunday. As the amount on hand decreased they made the beverage weaker and weaker, until the doctor laughingly declared that the snow flavored the water more than the coffee did. The lack of coffee hit the captain more than the others, for he loved his cupful, strong, black, and without sugar.

It was on the last day of March that they heard a noise outside and then came a faint hammering on their door. All leaped up and ran to open the barrier. When it had been forced back a distance of a foot, they beheld two miners there, so weak they could scarcely stand, much less speak. "Sumthin' to eat!" whispered one of them hoarsely, and the other echoed the word "Eat!" as being all he could say.

The two were taken into the cabin and warmed up, while Earl prepared a thin vegetable soup for them, that being best for their stomachs, according to the doctor. They could hardly swallow at first, and it was not until the following morning that they were strong enough to sit up and tell their stories. They had been wintering back of the woods, but starvation had driven them forth in an attempt to reach Dawson City for supplies. Their strength had failed them, they had lost their way, and here they were.

"Take care of us, and we'll pay you well," said one of the miners. "We've got over a thousand dollars in gold dust with us and ten thousand in dust and nuggets hidden up at the camp."

"I'm afraid your money won't count up here," replied Foster Portney, sadly. "We're almost as badly off ourselves. Yet I am willing to share what I have." A vote was taken, and the miners remained; and that made two more mouths to feed out of their scanty store.

The first week in April saw them reduced to next to nothing. The flour was gone, so was the bacon and the canned goods, and it was pork and beans and stewed dried apples twice a day and nothing more.

Every one looked haggard, and all felt that something must happen soon. Would spring ever come?

"Pork and beans enough to last about three days yet," said Foster Portney, as he surveyed the scanty store, with the others standing around. "Three days, and after that—" He did not finish, and a silence fell on the crowd. Were they to suffer the pangs of actual starvation, after all?

CHAPTER XXX.

LAST WASHINGS FOR GOLD.

JUST one day before their provisions gave out the skies brightened as if by magic and the sun came out warmly. They could scarcely believe their eyes, so sudden was the change. The snow was cleared away from the door, and every one lost no time in rushing out into the fresh air.

"This is living again!" cried Earl. And then he added: "Let us beat down a path to Wompole's cottage and see how he is faring."

The others agreed, and soon they had a trail to the next cabin, where an old Alaskan gold hunter had gone into quarters all by himself. Wompole was also out, and they shook hands. When questioned he said he had run out of everything but beans, dried peas, and some smoked salmon, and he agreed to let them have enough of his stores to last them three days longer.

"Winter is broke up now," he remarked. "An' I reckon thar ain't no doubt but wot ye kin git ter Dawson an' back, if ye try."

"And I shall try," said Foster Portney; and an hour later he and Captain Zoss started off on snowshoes which they had made during their many idle hours. Randy and Earl saw their uncle depart with much anxiety, but did nothing to detain him, for food they must have, and that appeared the only manner in which to obtain it.

"If we could only bring down a bird or something with the gun," said Earl, some time later, and then he climbed the cliff and beat a path to the first belt of timber. But though he thrashed around three hours, not a sign of game was to be discovered anywhere.

The night was cold, but not nearly as much so as other nights had been, and on the following day the mercury when held in the sun actually crawled up to ten degrees above zero. And so it kept gradually becoming warmer, until the snow started to melt and they knew for a certainty that the long and tedious winter was a thing of the past.

It took Foster Portney and Captain Zoss five full days to find their way to Dawson City and back again. The return for the larger portion of the way was made on dog sledges driven by Indians. They had found provisions very scarce and high in price in Dawson City, but had brought back enough to last a month. One of the Indians had also brought provisions for the two miners, this commission having been executed through Mr. Portney, and the next day the miners set off for their own cabin with many sincere thanks for the assistance which had been rendered them.

On the day the provisions came in, they celebrated by

having what Dr. Barwaithe called "a round, square meal." To be sure there was nothing but the plainest kind of food, but there was enough, and that was of prime importance.

After this they watched eagerly for the day to come when they might get to work again. A bargain had been struck all around, whereby the doctor and the captain were to work the single sluice box on the upper claim and have four-fifths of the findings, the other fifth going to Foster Portney for keeping them — the contract to hold good so long as the pair were content to remain in the present camp.

"The water is running in the gulch!" was the welcome announcement made by Earl one day, and all went down to see the thin stream, which soon became stronger. The snow was almost gone now, and the sand, gravel, and dirt which was exposed to the sun was quite free from frost. The picks, shovels, and other tools were brought out and cleaned up, and two days later found them at work as during the previous summer. It was marvellous how the seasons changed when once there was a start.

Before the end of the month Mr. Portney made another trip to Dawson City, and this time he took with him both Randy and Earl. They had settled that they should remain in the gulch until the first of August, and now they took back, by Indian carriers, enough provisions to last the camp until that time.

The stop in Dawson lasted two days, and the boys had a chance to walk about the town and see how it had improved. There were now at least twoscore of buildings, and several of them were quite pretentious. At the dock were two steamboats, both nearly free of the ice which had held them fast all winter.

In the town there was much news to be heard of the many wonderful strikes which had been made. Several had taken out over a hundred thousand dollars in dust and nuggets, and were waiting for navigation to open on the Yukon, that they might sail for home with their riches. No one who had accumulated a pile cared to remain in that forsaken country.

Just before they were to start for the gulch, Mr. Portney brought news of Tom Roland. The man had been captured at Circle City two months before, and the gold stolen from Cozzins taken from him. He had escaped from his temporary jail and fled to the mountains, and now his dead body had been found at the foot of a lofty cañon, down which he had most likely tumbled during the snowstorm which was then raging. It was a sad ending to a misspent life, and the boys could not help but shudder as they heard the story. They wondered what had become of Jasper Guardley, but nothing further was ever heard of that cowardly rascal.

By the first of June the gulch was as active as it had ever been during the previous summer, and the mosquitoes and flies were just as numerous and troublesome. No more finds of nuggets of large size were made, but the sluice boxes yielded heavy returns of dust, and all were very well content, and Dr. Barwaithe and Captain Zoss gave up all thoughts of leaving.

"We know what we have here," said the doctor, "and I am convinced that too much prospecting does not pay."

"An' besides, it's something ter be in company which is congenial," added the captain. "Over to the other claim it was nuthin' but fight the whole day long with yer neighbors about stake lines."

By the end of July the sand and gravel taken from the bedrock of Mosquito Hollow gulch had been disposed of, and now a month was given to a general clearing up of the dirt taken from half a dozen little hollows which lay on either side. It was terribly hot again, but the workers took their time over what they did, and often rested during the middle of the day. Three days before the first of September they were done.

"There, that settles it!" cried Foster Portney, as he flung down his shovel. "No more work for me until I have paid a visit to the States."

"Hurrah!" shouted Randy, and he gave his pick a whirl which sent it thirty feet off. "I'm just aching for a sight of civilization."

"And for an old-fashioned meal," added Earl.

Fred's eyes glistened, but he said nothing. He was

wondering what sort of a reception he would receive when he got home. He had sent on two letters from the gulch, but no answer had come back and there was no telling if the communications had reached their destination.

The next day was spent in the delightful task of counting up the proceeds of their venture. Of course it was impossible to calculate closely, yet they were conservative in their estimates, and in the end, when their nuggets and dust were turned over to the United States mint in San Francisco, they were not disappointed as to the check received in return.

The upper claim during the time it was worked by Dr. Barwaithe and Captain Zoss in the spring had yielded five thousand dollars. Of this, as per agreement, two thousand dollars went to the doctor, a like sum to the captain, and one thousand dollars to Foster Portney. Added to what they had made previously, the doctor and the captain now held a matter of nine thousand dollars' worth of gold between them. Not a fortune, but still a tidy sum, all things considered.

The Portneys, of course, had fared much better. The total yield of gold to them from start to finish footed up to fifty-two thousand dollars. Of this amount, as we know, one-half went to Earl and Randy, which gave the lads exactly thirteen thousand dollars apiece. Twenty-six thousand dollars was Foster Portney's share, but out of this he had been compelled to spend three thousand dollars in bringing the party up and keeping them, and he would have to spend nearly another thousand in getting them home.

During the early summer of the present year, Earl, Randy, and Foster Portney had held a private talk concerning the amount to be granted to Fred, and it had been decided that he should have an even thousand dollars, one half to come from the two boys' share and the other from their uncle. Fred's fare was also to be paid clear through to Basco. The lad, when told of this decision, said he was more than satisfied, as the amount of work he had been able to do had really been very small on account of frequent attacks of sickness.

"I can't stand the climate," he said. "And I shan't attempt to come up here again. If father will let me, I'll go to college and become a lawyer."

The doctor was going on to Dawson City to give up mining and establish himself in his profession, having become satisfied that he could do better at this than he could in working a claim. But the captain decided to remain where he was.

"I'm bound ter strike it rich some day," he said. "An' I'm goin' ter rustle till I do."

"I certainly hope you strike it rich," said Randy; for the pair were now greater friends than ever.

It was a warm, clear day when the party of five left the gulch, with their faces set toward Dawson City.

The Portneys had decided to return to the States by the way of the Yukon and the Pacific Ocean, and a voyage of five thousand miles still lay before them. They carried all their findings with them, and now the question arose,— having found so much gold, would they be able to get it out of this wild country in safety?

CHAPTER XXXI.

DOWN THE YUKON AND HOME.

Foster Portney knew that the regular terminus of travel on the Yukon steamboats was Fort Cudahy, which was situated forty-eight miles below Dawson City. But owing to the rush to the new gold fields, which was now stronger than ever, two small boats were making regular trips between these two points.

When the party reached Dawson City, now the scene of great activity, it was found they would have to wait a week before they could secure passage to Fort Cudahy, as the tickets for the two following trips were all sold. This wait, when they were impatient to get home, was not an agreeable one, yet it gave them a chance to look around the settlement and become better acquainted with the various persons who were there.

"Dawson is bound to grow," said the doctor, who had hired a room at the so-called hotel and hung out his sign on the day he arrived. "See, there are actually three streets already, two stores, three saloons, a barber shop, and a reading and pool room; and I understand that a fellow has just arrived who is going to open a clothing store, and another is on his way with medicines for a drug store. We are bound to boom!"

"'We' is good!" said Earl, with a laugh. "I guess you had better strike up a partnership with that druggist when he arrives."

"Not much, Earl! I'll put him in the way of getting the gold fever, and when he is ready to strike out, I'll buy his outfit and run the whole thing myself. I'm bound to make money." And it looked as if the doctor was right, for during their stay in Dawson City he had eleven calls for his services, for which he charged the fee of five dollars per call, which was moderate for that place.

At last came the day to part, and with a hearty hand-shake from the doctor the Portneys and Fred boarded the little side-wheeler *Alice*, and the long homeward trip was begun. The boat was crowded with returning miners, and as nearly all of them had struck gold, it was a happy congregation which spent the time in eating, drinking, smoking, playing cards, and "swapping yarns." "Swapping yarns" went on continually, and many were the wonderful stories told of great finds, perilous climbs, and escapes from starvation during the awful winter.

"I've made seventy thousand dollars, boys," said one elderly miner. "But I never did so much starving in my life, an' ten hosses couldn't drag me back to put in another such winter — hear me!"

"I'm with ye," said another; "leas'wise, I think I am. But thar's no tellin' wot I might do ef the gold fever struck me ag'in," he added reflectively.

Fort Cudahy was a small settlement on the Yukon, at the mouth of Clinton Creek. Just above the creek was another settlement, called Forty Mile. Between the stores in the two settlements there was a fierce rivalry, and consequently prices here were more reasonable than at Dawson City.

The party was fortunate in obtaining immediate passage to Fort Get There, on St. Michael's Island, which is situated sixty miles above the entrance to the Yukon. An offer was also made by the agent of the transportation company to take charge of their gold from there right on through to San Francisco, but as the commission for doing this would be fifteen per cent, this offer was declined.

"I think we can get it through," said Foster Portney. "At any rate, I am willing to risk it." And the boys agreed with him.

The next stop of importance was Circle City, of which the boys had heard through Mr. Portney. In former days Circle City had been the banner mining town on the upper Yukon, but now its glory was departed, for over three-quarters of its inhabitants had pulled up stakes and moved on to the Klondike district.

From Circle City the river, already broad, widened out to such an extent that it looked more like a lake than anything else. It was dotted with numerous islands, and the pilot of the boat had his head full with keeping track of the proper channel to pursue. The run was north to the ruins of Fort Yukon, the highest point gained by the mighty river upon which they were sailing.

From Fort Yukon the run was mostly to the southwestward, past the settlements of Shaman's, We Are, Nulato, and a dozen similar places, Indian villages, the home of fur traders, missionaries, and of fishers. At many of the places the main things to be seen were the totem poles stuck up in front of the Indian huts — poles of wood, curiously carved with hideous-looking images and undecipherable hieroglyphics.

At last St. Michael's Island was gained, and here they found themselves again in luck, for an ocean steamer was in waiting to take the passengers from the river boat. The transfer was made before nightfall, and at dawn of the day following the steamer started on her long voyage down Norton Sound, Bering Sea, and the Pacific Ocean to Seattle. But one stop was made, that at Dutch Harbor, on one of the Aleutian Islands, and then one glorious afternoon early in the fall they steamed through the Straits of San Juan de Fuca and swept into the grand harbor at Seattle.

"The United States at last!" cried Randy. "Oh my, how good civilization does look!"

"We don't know what we have at home until we miss it," said Fred, but in such a low tone that nobody heard him.

They stopped in Seattle two days, and then took steamer direct for San Francisco. The trip down the coast was an uneventful one. They were impatient to finish it, and a glad cry rang everywhere through the vessel when land was sighted and they ran through the Golden Gate.

A crowd was at the wharf to receive the latest news from the gold fields. "How are the diggings up there?" "Is there any show for a fellow staking a good claim?" "How much did you bring along?" "Is it true about provisions being scarce?" These and a hundred other questions went the rounds, as the fortunate ones came ashore. Foster Portney managed to keep the boys together and get them through the jam, and quarter of an hour later found them on the way to the mint with their precious burdens. Here they were given receipts for their nuggets and dust, and then they turned away with a big load lifted off their minds, for they knew that their fortunes were now safe.

And here properly ends the tale of the fortune hunters of the Yukon. How Fred Dobson returned home a penitent runaway, and how he was readily forgiven and later on allowed to study for college, I will leave my readers to imagine. As for Earl and Randy, there was nothing which called for their return to Basco, and they remained with their uncle in San Francisco until their gold was reduced to coin and they received a check on the treasurer of the United States for its value. Then they paid a visit to Colorado, remaining there until the following spring. During the winter a company was organized to work their claims by machinery, and early spring found them again in the land of gold. And there we will leave them, wishing them all the success that their pluck and industry deserve.

THE END.

www.ingramcontent.com/pod-product-compliance
Lightning Source LLC
Chambersburg PA
CBHW032138230426
43672CB00011B/2385